COOKI

THE OLDEST FOODS ON EARTH

AUSTRALIAN BUSH FOODS
RECIPES AND SOURCES

JOHN NEWTON

NEWSOUTH

A NewSouth book

Published by
NewSouth Publishing
University of New South Wales Press Ltd
University of New South Wales
Sydney NSW 2052
AUSTRALIA
newsouthpublishing.com

A catalogue record for this
book is available from the
National Library of Australia

ISBN   9781742237602 (Paperback)
        9781742238364 (ebook)
        9781742239262 (ePDF)

Design and illustrations Josephine Pajor-Markus
Cover design Luke Causby, Blue Cork
Cover images The cover designer was delighted to tell us that he sourced some of the
produce for the images from his local farmers' markets, and the pigface (karkalla) from
his local beach. Images, clockwise from top left: Pigface (Luke Causby), Tasmanian
pepperberry (*Adobe Stock*), Blue crayfish (*Adobe Stock*), Finger limes (Luke Causby),
Samphire (*Adobe Stock*), *Acacia Murrayana* (Wattle) seed pod (Maurice MacDonald,
Science Image), Quandongs (bottom: pxhere, top: Wikimedia), Lemon myrtle leaves
(Luke Causby) and Dried and crushed Tasmanian pepperberry leaves (Science Image).

CONTENTS

WE RESPECTFULLY ACKNOWLEDGE THE TRADITIONAL OWNERS
OF THE LAND AND THEIR ELDERS, PAST AND PRESENT.

ABOUT THE AUTHOR

JOHN NEWTON is a freelance writer, journalist and novelist. He writes
on food, eating, travel, farming and associated environmental issues. His
most recent books include *The Getting of Garlic*, *The Oldest Foods on Earth*
(which came third in the Gourmand World Cookbook Award for Best
Culinary History Book in 2017) and *Grazing: The ramblings and recipes of
a man who gets paid to eat*. In 2005 he won the Gold Ladle for Best Food
Journalist in the World Food Media Awards.

INTRODUCTION

Food has a culture. A history. A story.
It has a relationship and identity.

Mindy Woods, proud Bundjalung woman of the
Widjabul Wia-bul clan, chef and owner of Karkalla, Byron Bay.

When I first began writing about bush foods in 2015, all the suppliers and producers and all but a very small number of restaurants had non-Indigenous owners. As this recent statement from the website of the First Nations Bushfoods and Botanical Alliance Australia (FNBBAA)* points out, this is still the case:

> In 2019, Indigenous Australians represent fewer than 2% of the providers across the supply chain [while] nearly 98% of Aboriginal landowners aspire to be leaders in the bush food industry. In 2020, this is not acceptable, given that much of the industry relies on the supply of unprotected Indigenous knowledge and returns little to our people.

But in this new edition of *Cooking With the Oldest Foods on Earth* I can record that this is rapidly changing as more and more First Nations-owned producers, chefs

---

* The FNBBAA was established at a meeting that took place among 120 First Nations attendees at the inaugural Indigenous Native Foods Symposium in Sydney 2019.

and businesses move into the bush foods space.

Another tendency which I reported back then was the normalisation of the use of indigenous ingredients by top non–Indigenous chefs. Here's the way Quay's Peter Gilmore in Sydney explained it:

> It's not to make it [bush food] gimmicky, it's to incorporate it in a seamless way into the cuisine we're developing in Australia, which is multicultural Australian food. And there is no doubt that is happening.

And there is no doubt that is now happening all around the country. A search through the *Good Food Guide* 2020 reveals scores of examples: a peach Melba cake at Brisbane's Arc coated with finger lime, marron tail with a bush tomato and brown butter emulsion at Perth's Wildflower, Portobello mushrooms threaded on eucalyptus twigs at Sydney's Paperbark. I could go on.

In addition to merely incorporating bush foods, chefs like Attica's Ben Shewry, winner of the *Gourmet Traveller* 2020 Restaurant of the Year award, are seeking an understanding of the cultural context and history of these ingredients in dialogue with their suppliers.

That's the next step. For bush foods to become a mainstay of the Australian multicultural food scene it's important that Indigenous knowledge and participation is sought and, wherever possible, the complex seasonal and local associations of the foods used is referenced. I said wherever possible because it isn't always. We're often cooking in cities a long way from the origins of the foods being used. But the bottom line must remain respect for the ingredients, respect for their provenance and, wherever possible, sourcing from Indigenous producers.

INTRODUCTION

What do I mean by bush foods? There are, of course, local foods we have always eaten: oysters, crabs, rock crayfish, bugs, yabbies and marrons, and all the fish that swim around us. Many were familiar to the colonisers as they had been to First Nations peoples for millennia. And there were familiar game birds – varieties of duck and quail, for example.

But outside the familiar are an estimated 6000 edible plants, including 2400 fruiting trees in south-east Queensland alone, and 2000 truffles or subterranean mushrooms, mostly untasted. Of those 6000, non-Indigenous Australians currently use less than 50 – and cultivate around 20 for commercial sale.

Figures are hard to get, but it is estimated that the value of the bush foods industry is around $20 million annually: of which, a reminder, only 2 per cent goes to Indigenous producers.

While we should applaud the non-Indigenous chefs, restaurateurs and suppliers who kicked off a greater interest in bush foods, it's gratifying – and essential – to see more and more Indigenous businesses starting up. And just as gratifying to see the non-Indigenous businesses committing to supporting Indigenous producers. You'll find evidence of this in the Sources and resources section of this book, and in the recipes here from Indigenous cooks and chefs.

Why should you eat these foods? Firstly, for their unique flavours, then for their nutrient values. In recent years, research conducted into the nutrient content of bush food plants has confirmed that they are among the richest on the planet in the nutrients we need for good health. You want superfoods? Here they are. There are also native animals and birds that we could and should be eating and which, for a variety of reasons, we generally continue to ignore. We have a long way to go.

This book is for those of

you who want to understand more about the foods you're already using, and to encourage those new to bush foods to start incorporating them into your home cooking.

I want to be able to stand in a suburban street and smell 'roo being barbecued, riberries being simmered for sauce and jam, to know that wattleseed is being rolled into pavlova and finger lime caviar is being squirted onto oysters and fish, and into the evening gin and tonic. That is beginning, and the way it is spreading is straightforward.

We eat something at, say, Quay or Karkalla in Byron Bay. We love it and want to cook it at home. At the end of this book, I'll give you a list of people who can already supply you with much of what you want. But if we can't find it, we must pester our butchers/greengrocers/fishmongers and supermarkets until they stock it.

Don't be impatient. Remember, non-Indigenous Australians have ignored most of these foods since 1788 and the real interest began only twenty years ago.

The major difficulty for the home cook is still supply. Where do you get it? Retail has been very slow on the uptake, though there are signs of change. My local (Italian) greengrocer stocks finger limes. The big supermarkets are (still) flirting with the idea of stocking fresh indigenous produce: we've been waiting for this to happen since the first version of this book in 2019. In the meantime, we are doing our best to help you source what is available – and to encourage you to grow what you can't find.

At the end of the book, in addition to a Bibliography, there is an updated Sources and resources section – a list of businesses where you can find the ingredients you need – and a country-wide list of nurseries who stock bush food plants. But before we get into the food and the recipes, a few guidelines.

INTRODUCTION

Firstly, if you haven't had much experience with bush foods – herbs, fruits, and greens – you're going to encounter some very different flavours. They will be more intense, less sweet, tangier, even sour. There will be flavours you don't even have words for. In the Bibliography I've added the address for an AgriFutures report called 'Defining the Unique Flavours of Australian Native Foods'. It's worth a look. You can download a pdf for free or buy the book.

Secondly, a word of caution on foraging. Before you go out into the bush to pick your own, read the section entitled Foraging, dos and don'ts.

Finally, remember that these foods, like all foods, are seasonal: there's a section on the vastly different Indigenous concept of seasonality in the body of the book. And wherever possible, try to buy from a source that is either Indigenous owned or has close ties with Indigenous communities.

This book is a guide on how to source, select and cook with bush food ingredients. It's arranged by ingredient – I've chosen ten of the most popular and useful plant ingredients, and a selection of fish, seafood and macropods (kangaroos and wallabies) and one game bird. There is also a chapter dealing with grasses and rices, which are still in the research and development phase.

Interspersed between the ingredient chapters are a series of features on various aspects of bush foods for those with an interest in these significant additions to the their diet.

We hope this book is a step towards making the unique and remarkable produce of our land commonplace in your kitchen.

WATTLESEEDS

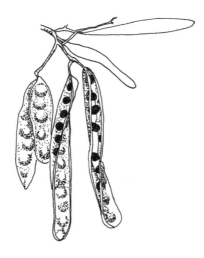

Wattleseeds are the edible seeds from any of the 120 species of Australian *Acacia* used as food by Indigenous Australians. But we'll stick to one – *Acacia victoriae* – which has an impressive list of common names: prickly wattle, elegant wattle, bramble wattle, gundabluey and narran among them.

A. victoriae is a shrub-like tree, with a number of trunks and long thin leaves. It has small, bulbous yellow flowers and long pods, like bean or carob pods, that contain the seeds. Wattleseeds from this variety have a nutty flavour with overtones of coffee and chocolate, and an aroma of crushed nuts and cereal.

NUTRITIONAL PROPERTIES

Wattleseeds contain calcium, zinc, magnesium, iron, potassium and other nutrients for good health. They are a low glycaemic carbohydrate and an excellent source of protein and fibre.

AVAILABLE FORMS

Wattleseeds are available whole, roasted and ground, or milled into a powder.

COOKING WITH WATTLESEEDS

Wattleseeds can be roasted and turned into a type of flour. They can be used to thicken sauces or casseroles, make a good ice-cream flavouring, or can be added to chocolate or desserts. Dry-roasted seeds are sometimes made into a beverage. Sprinkle the whole seeds through biscuits or flatbreads.

Pioneer chef Jean-Paul Bruneteau did most of the early work, along with scientist Vic Cherikoff, on adapting wattleseeds to the European diet. Bruneteau learnt that the essential flavour of wattle is only released when cooked with water, and he developed the Gundabluey mud recipe, on page 19, which can be used as a base for many wattleseed applications, including Bruneteau's celebrated pavlova on page 16. The seeds are popular mainly for their chocolate–vanilla flavour as well as their versatility.

· ·

FLEXIBLE BUILDING MATERIAL

The Anglo-Saxon word 'wattle' comes from the ancient house construction method. Branches and saplings were cut (from acacias) and woven onto wooden frames to create panels called wattles. These were then daubed with mud and dung to fill the gaps. A hut could be built in a day and dried out that night by burning a fire inside. Wattle-and-daub huts were common in the early days of European settlement in Australia. Various types of acacias were ideal for this work because the plants were plentiful and their cut stems were so flexible.

· ·

PAULA NIHOT

WATTLESEED AND PEPPERBERRY PASTA

Serves 4

The seed and gum of Australia's wattle have been harvested and used for thousands of years traditionally, providing nutritional and medicinal benefits in the harsh outback environment. I enjoy the flavour of the roasted and ground seed in savoury dishes, but my daughters like to add it to their cheesecake base. Whatever your preference, sweet or savoury, use wattleseed as a great flavour hit. Serve this pasta with Spicy mussels with bush tomato, aniseed myrtle and finger lime (see page 45). PN

1 teaspoon wattleseeds
½ teaspoon Tasmanian pepperberries
400 g plain flour
1 teaspoon olive oil
1 teaspoon water

1. In a non-stick frying pan over medium–low heat, lightly toast the wattleseeds and pepperberries until fragrant. Allow to cool slightly.
2. Place the toasted spices and the remaining ingredients in a food processor and process until the mixture resembles coarse breadcrumbs.
3. Gently press the mixture together to form a dough, then turn it out onto a lightly floured work surface. Knead for approximately 5 minutes.

4. Wrap the dough in plastic wrap, then set aside at room temperature for 20 minutes.
5. Cut the dough into quarters and, using a pasta machine, roll each piece through, folding and re-rolling, as you work your pasta into the desired thickness. If you do not have a pasta machine, the dough can be rolled and folded using a rolling pin – this will take more effort.
6. Use the pasta machine or a sharp knife to cut the pasta into your desired form.
7. Separate the pasta pieces and leave them to dry on a pasta-drying rack or a lightly floured clean tea towel.
8. Bring a pot of salted water to the boil. Add the pasta and cook for approximately 4 minutes.
9. Rinse and drain the pasta, place in bowls and serve with your desired sauce.

Note: You can also use the pasta dough to make lasagne sheets, rather than cutting it into thinner shapes.

Paula Nihot is a descendant of Susan, of the Namoi River, within the Gamillaraay language region. Paula has lived on the Gold Coast for over twenty years and currently works at the Yugambeh Museum on a range of language activation programs. She writes that 'the utilisation of Australian native produce, harvested from the home garden or neighbourhood, supports the consumption of varied nutritional content as well as the passing on of Aboriginal knowledge'.

'HARDLY ANYTHING FIT FOR MAN TO EAT'

Strictly speaking, the first Australian bush food eaten by Europeans in Australia was raw cycad seeds, eaten by the crew of Dutch explorer Willem de Vlamingh in Western Australia in 1697. According to their report on the meal, they were so ill that de Vlamingh wrote 'there was hardly any difference between us and death'. This is the first of many instances where explorers and visitors forgot to ask the Indigenous inhabitants how to prepare the ingredients!

Captain James Cook and the botanist Sir Joseph Banks are believed to be the first Europeans to successfully digest a meal made from Australian bush foods. Before detailing it, we should remind ourselves of Cook's opinion of the foods on offer in 'New Wales'.

In the journal of his first voyage around the world (1768–71) James Cook noted in his account of what he called New Wales, that 'The Land naturally produces hardly anything fit for Man to eat …' – a curious claim considering he was only here from April to August 1770 and barely spent any time ashore. And even more so if you read what Cook wrote about the foods he found in that very small portion of the land that he visited.

He acknowledges 'a few sorts of fruit' and describes what we now believe is the black plum or black apple (*Planchonella australis*). He then mentions taro, both the root and the leaves, before moving on to animals and seafood. First was the kangaroo, which he describes as 'very good eating', then lizards and snakes.

And 'land fowls' – the English, then as now, love to hunt game birds. He identified bustards, doves, quails, geese (more than likely magpie geese) and ducks among many others. Indeed, in his journal he wrote of the Australian bustard that 'it turned out an excellent bird, far the best … that we have eat since we left England'.

And finally fish – rockfish, mullet, bream, mackerel, leather jackets, stingrays – and shellfish such as oysters, cockles, clams, mussels, what he calls craw fish (rock lobsters) 'and a variety of other sorts'. Further up the coast he encountered the green turtle, which he opined was 'the finest … in the world'.

In spite of there being nothing fit to eat, Cook and Banks managed to put together a meal that was the first to be eaten (safely) by non-Indigenous people in Australia. Tetragon, known today as warrigal greens or New Zealand spinach, was noted, collected and eaten by Cook and Banks in 1770. On 6 May Cook wrote in his journal, 'We dined today upon the stingray and his tripe … We had with it a dish of the leaves of tetragonia cornuta boiled, which eat as well as spinage or very near it.'

Today, almost 250 years later, non-Indigenous Australians are discovering that there is indeed plenty fit to eat on this island continent. And still more to be rediscovered.

JEAN-PAUL BRUNETEAU

ROLLED WATTLESEED PAVLOVA

Serves 4–6

When making meringues of any sort it is imperative that the whisking bowls and whisks are not greasy. It is also vital that no speck of egg yolk is present in the whites, as even a minute amount of yolk is enough to prevent the whites from stiffening. An oven at 150°C is the precise temperature for the perfect pavlova. More or less than this heat will dramatically alter the result. Don't add too much of the Gundabluey mud, or it may curdle the cream. If you wish, you can use an emu egg. One emu egg is equivalent to 12 hen eggs, but there really is only enough to make one pavlova. The flavour isn't compromised. J-PB

50 g macadamia nuts, roasted
and unsalted
100 g hazelnuts, roasted
100 g pecan nuts, roasted
450 g caster sugar
1 heaped teaspoon ground
cinnamon

6 egg whites
1 teaspoon vinegar or strained
lemon juice
200 ml cream
2 tablespoons Gundabluey mud
(see page 19)

1. Preheat the oven to 150°C. To make the sugar crust, put the macadamia nuts in a food processor, then chop into large crumbs. Set aside. Repeat the process with the hazelnuts and pecan nuts and set aside.

WATTLESEEDS

2. Place 115 g of the caster sugar and the cinnamon in a food processor and blitz for 15 seconds. Add all the nuts and process for a further 20 seconds.
3. Line an open-ended Swiss roll tray with baking paper. Use a little water to fix the paper in position, on the underside of the paper only.
4. Whisk the egg whites with the vinegar or lemon juice until soft peaks form. Add half the remaining caster sugar gradually to the whites, whisking until the whites are stiff. Fold in the remaining nut-free sugar.
5. Empty the entire contents of the mixing bowl onto the prepared tray in one clean sweep, using a rubber spatula – this helps keep air pockets to a minimum. Spread the mixture evenly over the tray, using a gooseneck spatula if you have one.
6. Sprinkle the sugar crust mixture evenly over the meringue. Bake in the oven for 20–22 minutes.
7. Remove the meringue from the oven, place a clean tea towel or a large sheet of baking paper over the top, then invert it onto a cake rack. Allow to cool.
8. Trim the four sides of the pavlova with a serrated knife and carefully remove the baking paper.
9. Whip the fresh cream until it starts to thicken. Add the Gundabluey mud and continue to whip until stiff.
10. Spread the cream evenly over the meringue and roll the pavlova like a Swiss roll.

Jean-Paul Bruneteau is a French–Australian chef and a leader in the development of an authentic Australian cuisine. In his kitchen at Rowntrees, and then Riberries, both restaurants in Sydney, Australian bush foods were skilfully incorporated into a European context. This recipe is from Jean-Paul Bruneteau's 1996 book, Tukka: Real Australian Food. *If you can find a copy, buy it.*

MACADAMIA NUT

Until recently about the only bush food regularly eaten by Australians was the macadamia nut, first farmed in Hawaii. In spite of being a food prized by Indigenous Australians for thousands of years, it was only 'discovered' by English botanist Allan Cunningham in 1828 and named (after Australian scientist Dr John Macadam) in 1857. It was first planted commercially near Lismore in 1882, two years after seeds were first sent to Hawaii. Macadamia farms boomed in northern New South Wales in the 1980s. Its popularity in those early days was probably because it was not sold under any of its Indigenous names, which included *gyndl* or *jindilli* and *boombera*.

JEAN-PAUL BRUNETEAU

....

GUNDABLUEY MUD

Makes about 1 litre

The 'mud' is made through the absorption of water by the roasted ground wattleseeds over a very low flame. It is important never to boil the seeds, as the flavour becomes 'dusty' and bitter. The mud stores well in the fridge for up to a week if well covered and sealed with plastic wrap. It can also be used to make wattleseed ice cream. J-PB

110 g roasted ground wattleseeds
600 ml water
pinch of salt

1. Put the wattleseeds, water and salt in a stainless steel frying pan. Simmer until reduced by two-thirds, or until the grounds meet the surface of the liquid. Do not boil.
2. Process the cooked grounds in a blender at high speed until they become a smooth mud.
3. Scrape the contents of the blender into a clean container, allow to cool, then seal. Store in the fridge until you need it.

LEMON MYRTLE

The leaves of the remarkable lemon myrtle, *Backhousia citriodora*, which are the main part we use, contain high levels of citral – the fragrant liquid in citrus fruit. Lemon myrtle contains 90–98 per cent compared to 10 per cent in a lemon. This explains the wonderful taste and aroma that lemon myrtle leaves give to food and drinks. It has an aroma of creamy lime and lemon, with notes of menthol and strong lemon/lemongrass flavour, sweet and cooling on the palate.

In the rainforest, *B. citriodora* can grow up to 20 metres in height and has long hanging branches of soft green leaves with cream flowers in autumn. It occurs naturally in the wetter coastal areas of New South Wales, and in the higher rainforests in Queensland.

NUTRITIONAL PROPERTIES

Lemon myrtle contains lutein, a vitamin that plays an important role in eye health. It's also an excellent source of folate, vitamin A, vitamin E and many essential oils. It's a good source of calcium for vegans and has high levels of antioxidants. Citral has powerful antimicrobial and antifungal properties, which is why it's often used in soaps or shampoo or even cleaning products.

AVAILABLE FORMS

Lemon myrtle leaves are available fresh and dried, or ground into a powder or, the best way of all, from your own tree (see Grow your own, pages 133–36).

COOKING WITH LEMON MYRTLE

Lemon myrtle is wonderful for the lemon or lemongrass flavour it gives to fish, chicken, ice cream, cheesecake or sorbet and it's a great substitute for lemongrass in stir-fries. You can sprinkle powdered lemon myrtle leaves on anything from pumpkin soup to salads.

If you are lucky enough to have access to a tree, you can use the whole dried leaves – pick the older darker leaves for their flavour. Remember that the whole leaf will have little aroma until it is scrunched, powdered or until heat is applied.

Add a leaf or a sprinkle of powder – half a teaspoon per 500 g of meat – when steaming or roasting fish or chicken. Use it sparingly and, when adding it to a dish such as a stir-fry for example, add it towards the end of the cooking, as overcooking diminishes the lemon flavour and can bring out harsh eucalyptus tones.

• • • • • • • • •

LEMON MYRTLEADE

During World War II, there was a shortage of lemon essence, so the Australian soft drink company Tarax made their lemonade using lemon myrtle. What a pity they stopped.

• • • • • • • • •

JILL DUPLEIX

CRISP-FRIED PRAWNS WITH ONION RINGS AND LEMON MYRTLE SALT

Serves 4

Fresh tiger prawns coated in Japanese tempura batter are deep-fried until crisp and served with onion rings and a dipping salt of lemon myrtle. It's a feast that comes from our long-standing love of Asian flavours, growing recognition of bush spices – and a national passion for 'fish and chips'. JD

8 large or 12 medium raw prawns
2 onions, peeled
2 teaspoons ground lemon myrtle
2 teaspoons crushed sea salt
vegetable oil, for deep-frying
2 tablespoons cornflour or rice
    flour

Batter
1 egg yolk
150 ml ice-cold sparkling water
125 g plain flour, sifted

LEMON MYRTLE

1. Peel and devein the prawns, leaving the tails intact.
2. Slice the onions, divide into rings and pat dry with paper towel (use the larger rings, the inner ones are too small).
3. Mix the lemon myrtle with the salt and set aside.
4. Heat the vegetable oil in a heavy-based frying pan or deep-fryer to 170°C.
5. To make the batter, beat the egg yolk, add the ice-cold water and lightly mix with chopsticks. Add the flour all at once, and very lightly mix, leaving it totally clumpy-lumpy.
6. Lightly coat two prawns in cornflour, brushing off the excess, then dip them in the batter and thickly coat. Gently lower the prawns into the hot oil and cook until lightly golden and puffed.
7. Drain well and repeat with the remaining prawns and the onion rings. Scatter with the lemon myrtle salt or serve the salt alongside for dipping.

Jill Dupleix is a food writer and cookbook author whose conversion to Australian bush foods has been profound. 'It's been a journey of discovery for me, as a home cook, to play with what is effectively a whole new box of spices, dried fruits and fresh wild greens in my own backyard. It's taken a few years, but I now actively prefer warrigal greens to spinach and kangaroo meat to venison. I turn to lemon myrtle and dried [mountain] pepper leaves instead of bay leaves for stocks, infusions and marinades, and add bush tomatoes to my chutneys.'

PAULA NIHOT

MACADAMIA-CRUMBED FISH FILLETS WITH LEMON MYRTLE

Serves 8

My dad, Tommy, loved to fish. When beach fishing, Dad would always come home with a feed of whiting. Mum grew a macadamia nut tree in our backyard. Fish and macadamia nuts are a great childhood memory and a perfect culinary combination. PN

Serve the fish with a salad and mango salsa, or with Burnt butter, bunya, zesty green beans and pepperberry (see page 34).

100 g macadamia nuts, chopped
100 g breadcrumbs made from
    Turkish bread
50 g coconut flakes
100 g coconut or plain flour
ground Himalayan rock salt
ground Tasmanian pepperberry

2 eggs
1 teaspoon Dijon mustard
1 tablespoon finely chopped fresh
    lemon myrtle leaf
8 fresh trag jewfish (see Note) or
    whiting fillets
olive oil, for shallow-frying

LEMON MYRTLE

1. On a flat plate mix the chopped macadamia nuts, Turkish breadcrumbs and coconut flakes.
2. Place the flour in a mixing bowl and season with the salt and pepperberry.
3. Gently whisk the eggs, mustard and lemon myrtle in a small bowl.
4. Pat the fish fillets dry with paper towel and dust them in the flour mix.
5. Dip the flour-dusted fish into the egg mix, coating well.
6. Place a fish fillet on the macadamia nut mix and spoon the mixture over the fish to coat the top, pressing the chopped nuts in firmly. Place the fish on a plate, then repeat with the remaining fish fillets.
7. Pour enough olive oil in a frying pan over medium heat to shallow fry. When the oil is hot, add the crumbed fish fillets and shallow-fry the fish until golden brown, 2 minutes. Turn and cook for a further 2 minutes, until golden brown on the underside. Add more oil if the first side has soaked up all the oil.
8. Transfer the cooked fish to paper towel to drain.
9. Serve the fish hot with the accompaniments of your choice.

Note: Trag jewfish or teraglin is a Queensland Gold Coast fish; mulloway is a good substitute.

REBECCA SULLIVAN

LEMON MYRTLE, DAVIDSON PLUM AND LIMONCELLO TRIFLE

Serves 8

*A bush-food take on a traditional English dessert gives it new
life and added zing from the Davidson and Illawarra plums. It's a
dessert you can make in the morning and serve at night.*

100 g Davidson plums (fresh or
    frozen)
100 g Illawarra plums (fresh or
    frozen)
4 Victorian or red plums
100 ml orange juice
zest of 1 orange
2 tablespoons sugar
1 whole homemade or store-
    bought sponge cake, or
    1 packet sponge finger biscuits
    (savoiardi/ladyfingers)

180 ml boiling water
1 tablespoon ground lemon myrtle
150–200 ml limoncello
500 ml custard, homemade or
    store-bought
500 ml thickened cream
2 tablespoons icing sugar, sifted
edible flowers, to garnish

1. Halve the Davidson plums and discard the stones. The Illawarra
plums have very small stones, so you can use them whole and
remove the stones later. Put all the plums in a small saucepan, along
with the orange juice, zest and sugar and bring to the boil. Reduce
the heat and simmer gently until the plums are falling apart. Leave
to cool.

2. If using a sponge cake, cut it into 2 cm slices. Layer the cake slices or sponge finger biscuits in the base, and a little way up the sides, of a serving bowl.
3. In a bowl, mix the boiling water and ground lemon myrtle. Add the limoncello then pour the mixture over the cake or biscuits in the bowl. (You can add more or less limoncello depending on how soggy you like the cake.) Push the cake or biscuits down to soak up the liquid.
4. Spoon in the cooled plum mixture. Next pile on the custard.
5. Whip the cream with the sifted icing sugar until thick. Add the cream on top of the custard, garnish with edible flowers and serve immediately or chill first.

Rebecca Sullivan and her partner, Damien Coulthard from Adnyamathanha Country, together created the food company Warndu. It is listed in Sources and resources.

. . . .

ILLAWARRA PLUM

The Illawarra plum grows on the tall brown pine (*Podocarpus elatus*) in two segments, a hard external and inedible seed and the larger purple-fleshed fruit. It is native to eastern New South Wales and Queensland. Unusually for native fruit, it is richly sweet, with an abundance of sticky sugars. What makes it unique and Australian is its plummy pine flavour. Its antioxidant levels are seven times that of blueberries, the basis for measurement of nutrients in other foods. The plums are used for jams, conserves, desserts, sauces and beverages.

. . . .

NATIVE SARSAPARILLA

I've included native sarsaparilla, *Smilax glyciphylla*, for its history, its flavour as a tea, and because it was the first bush foods plant I identified in the wild (with help from bush foods authority Vic Cherikoff).

In 2000, I joined Cherikoff on a foraging trip into a nondescript patch of sclerophyll forest alongside a busy section of Pittwater Road in Sydney. About 200 metres in we were surrounded by edible plants, ready to eat or waiting for their season, including the sarsaparilla plant. We ate the sweet young red leaves, which taste like liquorice, cola or aniseed – an unforgettable flavour.

In the early days of the colony, native sarsaparilla was one of the few bush food plants used enthusiastically by the British. They missed their tea and this plant was a good substitute. It continued to be valued as a tea until the late 19th century. You can pick your own for tea – it grows naturally from Cape York Peninsula to south-east New South Wales – or buy tea from suppliers listed at the end of the book.

TASMANIAN PEPPERBERRY

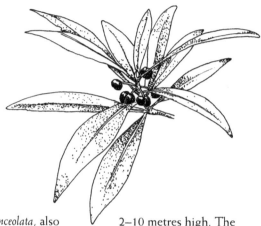

Tasmannia lanceolata, also known as Tasmanian or mountain pepperberry, or mountain pepper, is the most popular of the Australian native peppers, another being Dorrigo pepper, *T. stipitata*. There are seven species of *Tasmannia* in Australia, all found in mountainous regions from Cape York to Tasmania. Here I'll concentrate on *T. lanceolata*.

Tasmanian pepperberry is a bushy compact shrub, 2–10 metres high. The leaves are thin, green and 5–20 centimetres long with wavy edges. The plants are either male or female. Both sexes have small cream-coloured flowers with narrow petals. The male flower has many stamens; the female flower has a two-lobed ovary. The pea-sized berries grow in clusters and can be coloured either a pinkish white or a purplish black, with a deep furrow on one side.

The pepperberry was introduced to the European palate at the Fifth Symposium of Australian Gastronomy in 1990 by Stephen Harris, chief botanist with the Tasmanian Department of Parks, Wildlife and Heritage. Since then it has been cultivated and has become a popular item, prized for its pungent, aromatic heat. The crushed leaves of the tree can also be used as a spice.

NUTRITIONAL PROPERTIES

The compound that produces the heat in the pepperberry fruit and leaves, polygodial, is antimicrobial and antifungal. Both leaves and berries are high in folate, zinc, magnesium, manganese and antioxidants. There are also medium levels of iron.

AVAILABLE FORMS

Whole or crushed peppercorns, whole or powdered leaf.

COOKING WITH PEPPERBERRY

If you love heat, you will love this spice. The berry's heat is somewhere between pepper and chilli, but much more complex. It is almost fruit–candy sweet in both aroma and effect on the palate but has a lingering tongue-numbing heat that increases and lasts some minutes. Use it sparingly and experiment with quantities. You can buy the berries fresh or brined. If brined, wash the brine off them thoroughly. They are at their best when used in slow-cooked stews, soups and even curries, as their heat gives way to their unique flavour. The dark berries also infuse a rich plum colour to sauces and you can add them to your vinaigrettes.

The berries combine well with lemon myrtle and can be made into a sauce, which teams beautifully with kangaroo or beef – it's great on a steak.

The leaf, usually supplied as a powder, should also be used cautiously, not as you would a black or a white pepper but in the sparing way you add cayenne pepper. Add it to vinaigrettes.

JEAN-PAUL BRUNETEAU

....

PEPPERBERRY SAUCE

Makes 800 ml

*To make the perfect sauce for kangaroo and wallaby, the veal stock
and glaze must be prepared ahead of time. Reducing a skimmed,
strained and clarified veal stock over the lowest of heats is a
recommended culinary component of sauce-making, replacing flour
or starch thickeners. J-PB*

*Serve with any kangaroo or wallaby recipe, but especially
with Roast rump of kangaroo (see page 111).*

Veal stock and glaze

2 kg veal knuckles
1 onion, quartered
1 carrot, roughly chopped
1 celery stalk, chopped
2 bay leaves
5 litres water

The sauce

1 teaspoon olive oil
2 tablespoons fresh pepperberries
(mountain pepper) or well-
rinsed pepperberries in brine,
roughly chopped
500 ml cream sherry
1 litre veal stock (from method
opposite)
120 ml veal glaze (from method
opposite)

TASMANIAN PEPPERBERRY

Veal stock and glaze

1. Place all the ingredients into a large saucepan or stockpot and simmer for 2 to 3 hours.
2. Skim any scum from the surface of the stock then strain the stock into a bowl. Reserve 1 litre of the stock and return the remaining stock to the saucepan.
3. On the lowest of heats reduce the stock in the saucepan to 180 ml. The glaze should have a jam-like consistency.

The sauce

1. Heat the olive oil in a frying pan over medium heat, add half the pepperberries and fry a little.
2. Add the sherry to the pan and flame.
3. Add the reserved 1 litre of veal stock to the pan then add the glaze.
4. Simmer to a sauce consistency, reducing by at least half.
5. Add the remaining pepperberries. Alternatively, reserve them for serving with the meat.
6. Taste and add salt if required.

PAULA NIHOT

BURNT BUTTER, BUNYA, ZESTY GREEN BEANS AND PEPPERBERRY

Serves 4

*Paula tells us that 'the Bunya Pine (*Araucaria bidwillii*) grows in many parks and gardens throughout south-east Queensland. Bunya nuts taste wonderful with a little butter and garlic, are great in pesto and if I have any roasted ones left over (after the kids and their dad have smelt them cooking in the oven), I put them in the food processor to make bunya meal. You can use bunya meal just like flour.'*

45 g unsalted butter
2 cloves garlic, finely chopped
10 bunya nuts, chopped
500 g green beans, trimmed and blanched

2 finger limes, zest and caviar
ground Himalayan rock salt
ground Tasmanian pepperberry

1. Place the butter and garlic in a frying pan over medium–low heat. Cook for around 2 minutes. Add the bunya nuts and continue to cook for 2–3 minutes until the butter is dark golden and has a nutty aroma.
2. Turn off the heat and add the drained green beans and the zest of one finger lime. Mix through. Season with salt and pepper to taste.
3. Sprinkle finger lime caviar and remaining zest on top of the buttery beans.

BUNYA NUTS

The bunya nut comes from the Bunya Bunya pine (*Araucaria bidwillii*, previously *Pinus petriana*) a towering tree with a straight trunk and dark green leathery sharp-tipped leaves. The nut is actually the seed found inside the green, rounded cones. The bunya bunya is a rainforest tree growing in south-east and north-east Queensland.

This was a very important food for the local Indigenous people, especially the Waka Waka and Gubi Gubi whose name for the trees was *bon-yi* pronounced bon-yee. In what was probably Australia's largest Indigenous event, diverse tribes – up to thousands of people – once travelled great distances (from as far as Charleville, Dubbo, Bundaberg and Grafton) to celebrate the harvest of the nut, conduct trade and discuss regional issues.

The nuts can be eaten raw but are better roasted, and when boiled can be processed into nutmeal which can be added to bread mixtures. They can also be used for flavouring batters and, with cream, can be used as a pastry base. Bunya nuts are scarce as I write, but will become a more important and available food down the line.

The nutritional content of the bunya nut is 40 per cent water, 40 per cent complex carbohydrates, 9 per cent protein and 2 per cent fat. It is also gluten free, making bunya nut flour a substitute for people with gluten intolerance.

FIONA PORTEOUS

··

MOUNTAIN PEPPER TOFU

Serves 4

*I found this recipe and adapted it to use mountain pepperberry
instead of black pepper. It's delicious and light, and all
deep-fried and crunchy. FP*

150 g butter

12 small French shallots (350 g in
total), thinly sliced

8 fresh red chillies (fairly mild
ones), thinly sliced (seeded for
less heat if desired)

12 garlic cloves, crushed

3 tablespoons chopped fresh root
ginger

3 tablespoons sweet soy sauce
(kecap manis)

3 tablespoons light soy sauce

1 tablespoon dark soy sauce

2 tablespoons caster sugar

4 tablespoons coarsely crushed
Tasmanian pepperberries (use
a mortar and pestle or a spice
grinder)

16 small thin spring onions, cut
into 3 cm segments

plain steamed jasmine rice, to
serve

Crunchy tofu

800 g firm tofu (see Note)

cornflour, for dusting

vegetable oil, for frying

1. To make the crunchy tofu, cut the tofu into cubes about 3 x 2 cm.
   Toss them in the cornflour and shake off the excess.
2. Pour enough vegetable oil into a large frying pan or wok to come
   5 mm up the sides, then heat over medium–high heat until the oil
   is hot. Add the tofu to the hot oil in small batches and fry until the

cubes have a thin golden crust. As they are cooked, transfer them to paper towel. It doesn't matter if they cool down at this stage as they'll be reheated later.

3. Remove the oil and any sediment from the pan or wok. Put the butter in the pan and melt it over medium–low heat.
4. Add the shallots, chillies, garlic and ginger to the pan and sauté for about 15 minutes, stirring occasionally, until the ingredients have turned shiny and are totally soft. Watch to ensure they don't overcook.
5. Meanwhile, mix the soy sauces and sugar in a small bowl and stir until the sugar has dissolved.
6. When the shallots, chillies, garlic and ginger are soft and shiny, add the mixed soy sauces and sugar to the pan and stir.
7. Add the crushed mountain pepperberry to the pan and stir it through.
8. Add the tofu to the sauce and stir for about a minute, until warmed through.
9. Finally, stir in the spring onions.
10. Serve hot with plain steamed jasmine rice.

Note: Try to use quite a firm, relatively dry non-silken tofu to avoid the tofu breaking up.

Fiona Porteous is one half (with partner Peter Micallef) of Bent Shed Produce, where they grow bush foods and create products from it. Fiona is also a gifted home cook. Her practical hints on using these ingredients are scattered throughout this book. You'll find Fiona and Peter's website in Sources and resources.

A PREHISTORIC SURVIVOR

Gondwana was the name given to the southernmost of the two continents – the other being Laurasia – that were once part of one supercontinent called Pangaea, which existed from approximately 500 to 200 million years ago. Around 200 million years ago, Gondwana separated from Laurasia and drifted further south. It consisted of today's Antarctica, South America, Africa, Madagascar and Australia, as well as the Arabian Peninsula and the Indian subcontinent, which later moved north. There they were, all stuck together, crawling across the southern hemisphere and creeping into the northern hemisphere.

Australian soils are ancient and are generally low in fertility and organic matter. This makes life difficult for today's farmers and gardeners. It also made life difficult for the flora that grew here, which, in the long run, proved a good thing.

But it was climate that provided the most profound influence. Australia is the world's second-driest continent – after Antarctica – with an average mean annual rainfall below 600 millimetres over 80 per cent of the continent, and below 300 millimetres over 50 per cent, at the time of writing. The average January temperature over most of the country exceeds 30°C, but overnight frosts are common inland and it gets cold in the south.

What has this got to do with plant nutrients? In a word: stress.

With such extremes of climate, plants need to protect themselves. 'Plants are stressed a lot,' Dr Izabela Konczak, who has studied native edible fruits, herbs and spices at the CSIRO notes. 'The elevated level of compounds in the plants helps plant cells to survive. Also, soil conditions and the whole microclimate environmental factors would contribute.'

One food plant combines both Gondwanan and climatic influences. *Tasmannia lanceolata* is the tree that produces the Tasmanian pepperberry and leaf. Dr Konczak says: 'It is a very aromatic native pepper which was developed under the Antarctic climate' when Australia was attached to Gondwana. 'It had to protect itself from the cold and so developed a huge number of very different types of chemicals.' How many?

The leaf alone contains alphapinene, sabinene, beta-pinene, p-cymene, limonene, beta-phellandrene, 1,8-cineole, terpinolene, linalool, alpha-terpineol, piperitone, alpha-cubebene, eugenol, alpha-copaene, methyl eugenol, alpha gurjunene, caryophyllene, aromadendrene, germacrene-D, bicyclogermacrene, calamenene, cadina-1,4-diene, elemol, palustrol, spathulenol, guaiol, 220 MW sesquiterpene, 218 MW sesquiterpene 1, drimenol, polygodial and other unidentified volatiles.

Think of that the next time you cook with Tasmanian pepperberry or sprinkle the leaves on a dish. The plant is rich in the nutrients we need for our health.

BUSH TOMATO

There are several indigenous plants from the genus *Solanum*, which makes them relatives of the potato, tomato and eggplant and they are often referred to as bush tomatoes. The most popular of these, *Solanum centrale*, is also known as the desert raisin. This plant was described by Alice Springs botanist, Peter Latz, as 'probably the most important of all the central Australian plant foods'.

Native to Central and Western Australia, bush tomatoes grow on a shrubby plant with pale green or greyish leaves, which feel furry to the touch. The fruits look a little like small unripe tomatoes and are pale yellow when ripe. Before picking, they are left to dry on the branch, which reduces the level of harmful alkaloids and intensifies their flavour.

When dried and powdered, bush tomatoes are called by their Alyawarre name, *akudjura*, and in this form are used as a spice that has a caramel or sundried tomato flavour. It's best used sparingly in this form as too much will cause the pleasant flavour to be dominated by the bitter and sharp end of the flavour spectrum.

NUTRITIONAL PROPERTIES

Bush tomatoes contain medium levels of antioxidants, vitamin E, zinc and calcium, and are a rich source of folate, magnesium, iron and potassium. They are also a good source of selenium, which is necessary for antioxidant enzymes to function. Some Indigenous communities use them to treat toothache.

AVAILABLE FORMS

Whole fresh fruit, dried and powdered.

COOKING WITH BUSH TOMATO

This fruit, once dried and powdered, is a highly versatile spice. Once you have akudjura in your kitchen, you'll wonder how you ever got along without it. But be warned – it's one of those spices where less is more.

Rub a shoulder of lamb with akudjura and olive oil, flavour bread or damper with akudjura alone or add rosemary and thyme. It can flavour casseroles or be rubbed onto meats before grilling along with coriander, wattleseed and lemon myrtle. It works well with cheese, eggs, salmon and stronger-flavoured white or game meats. You can also use it in dukkah or crustings on meat. In his book *Wild Foods*, Vic Cherikoff reckons it makes a good substitute for fish sauce (great for vegans!). Basically, get it into your kitchen and experiment.

• •

WESTERN DESERT USE

Between 1966 and 1967, anthropologist Richard A Gould lived with a group of thirteen Nyatunyatjara (alternate English spelling Ngaanyatjarra) people in the harsh climate of the Gibson Desert, north of Warburton and around 1500 kilometres north-east of Perth. At the time, the Western Desert was one of the last regions of the world to support groups of people living entirely on the uncultivated resources of the land. Gould's visit coincided with the last months of a severe drought.

He observed that the diet of the Nyatunyatjara was primarily vegetarian and at least 90 per cent of the time women provided 95 per cent of the food for the group.

He recorded women gathering two plant foods: kampurarpa, a small green tomato-like fruit and ngaru (both from the *Solanum* genus) and pounding them into a paste. The paste could be eaten fresh or rolled into large balls, which could be dehydrated and stored until wanted.

• •

RAYMOND KERSH

PARSNIP AND BUSH TOMATO SOUP

Serves 6–8

*This is a deceptively simple soup combining the sweetness
of parsnip with the almost umami savoury flavour of akudjura.
It shows the versatility of akudjura.*

1 onion, roughly chopped
3 garlic cloves, roughly chopped
1 teaspoon akudjura (dried and
 powdered bush tomato)
750 g parsnips, roughly chopped

250 g potatoes, roughly chopped
150 g butter
2 litres beef, chicken or vegetable
 stock
salt and pepper, to taste

1. Sauté the onion, garlic, akudjura, parsnips and potatoes in the butter
   until all the ingredients are well softened.
2. Add the stock, bring to the boil, then reduce the heat and simmer for
   10–15 minutes until the potatoes are well cooked.
3. Remove the soup from the heat, transfer it to a blender or food
   processor and purée. Season the soup with salt and pepper, then
   strain it back into the saucepan. Return to the heat to ensure it is
   warm before serving.

*Chef Raymond Kersh and front of house Jennice (his sister) presided over a
series of Edna's Table restaurants in Sydney, introducing countless Australians
and visitors from other countries to the unique flavours of bush foods.*

RAYMOND KERSH

....

BUSH TOMATO CHUTNEY

Makes about 1 kg

I've been doing this for years. For a delicious tangy and versatile chutney, just put all the ingredients together and boil them. Use it as you'd use any chutney. RK

500 g tomatoes, peeled and
  chopped
500 g onions, diced
2 tablespoons akudjura (dried and
  powdered bush tomato)
1 cup brown sugar
250 ml apple cider vinegar

1 tablespoon English mustard
  powder
1 tablespoon salt
1 teaspoon cayenne pepper
1 tablespoon curry powder
1 tablespoon beef booster
2 tablespoons cornflour

1. Put all the ingredients (except the cornflour) in a non-reactive saucepan, such as stainless steel. Bring to the boil and cook for approximately 20 minutes.
2. Add the cornflour and continue to boil for an extra 10 minutes.
3. Pour into sterilised glass jars and store in the fridge for up to two months.

PAULA NIHOT

SPICY MUSSELS WITH BUSH TOMATO, ANISEED MYRTLE AND FINGER LIME

Serves 4

Another simple but simply perfect recipe from Paula, whose use of bush foods is rooted in her upbringing and family traditions. She recommends serving it over Wattleseed and pepperberry pasta (see page 12).

2 tablespoons olive oil

1 red onion, diced

4 garlic cloves, thinly sliced

4 red chillies, thinly sliced

10 fresh aniseed myrtle leaves, finely chopped

3 fresh bush tomatoes, chopped

400 g tin of crushed tomatoes

250 ml dry white wine

250 ml chicken stock

15 bunya nuts, halved

2 tablespoons apple cider vinegar

1 tablespoon brown sugar

1 kg mussels, scrubbed and debearded

5 finger limes, to serve

ground Tasmanian pepperberry, to taste

1. In a large saucepan, heat the olive oil over medium–high heat. Add the onion, garlic, chilli, aniseed myrtle and bush tomatoes and sauté for 3–4 minutes, or until soft.
2. Stir in the crushed tomatoes, wine, stock and bunya nuts. Add the apple cider vinegar and brown sugar. Mix all the ingredients and bring to the boil.
3. Add the mussels and cover the pan with a lid, cooking for 3–4 minutes. Shake the pan every 2 minutes to redistribute the mussels and encourage them to open. Discard any unopened mussels. Season with salt and pepper to taste.
4. Before serving, break open the finger limes and squeeze the caviar over the mussels. Sprinkle with a little ground pepperberry.

INDIGENOUS SEASONS

The four seasons of Europe do not begin to describe the variations across Australia's vast land. But for over 60 000 years, the original inhabitants have adopted seasons based upon acute observation of their country. Here is just one of the many Indigenous seasonal cycles to give you the idea.

Aboriginal groups throughout the tropical north of Australia have the same seasonal cycle as the Yolnu (the Aboriginal group of north-east Arnhem Land, sometimes spelt Yolngu). Their seasons are:

DHULUDUR
The pre-wet season in October–November

BÄRRA'MIRRI
The growth season in December–January

MAYALTHA
The flowering season in February–March

MIDAWARR
The fruiting season in March–April, including

NGATHANGAMAKULINGAMIRRI
The two-week harvest season in April

DHARRATHARRAMIRRI
The early dry season in May–July, including

BURRUGUMIRRI
The time of the birth of sharks and stingrays –
three weeks in July–August

RARRANDHARR
The main dry season in August–October.

The range of foodstuffs available to the Yolnu people across these seasons is remarkable, making our European choices appear skimpy. Even in the pre-wet season, Dhuludur, one of the least prolific, there is much to choose from.

Some of the foods available during Dhuludur include the native grape, long and round yam, the new growth of the finger bean and the giant waterlily. As the waterholes shrink early in the season, magpie geese flock to the remaining water, making them easy prey for hunters. When the waterholes begin to fill, the whistling duck, Pacific black duck and radjah shelduck all come home to build their nests to breed, which means they are fat.

DAVIDSON PLUM

The only native fruit that could mount a State of Origin competition, *Davidsonia jerseyana* is often called the New South Wales plum because that's where it originated, growing in rainforests between Mullumbimby and Murwillumbah. *D. jerseyana* fruits emerge from the trunk between November and February and look very much like Damson plums. Today, it's mainly cultivated rather than found in the wild. Inevitably, as is the Australian way, the fruit are called 'Davos'.

Davidsonia pruriens from Queensland bears larger fruit, also on the trunk or higher branches, covered in irritant hairs that need to be washed off. The hairy Davo (as it is known locally) grows all through the wet tropics, on the Atherton Tablelands, the Daintree and between Innisfail and Cooktown. While it can fruit any time of the year, it's most prolific from April to October.

D. *pruriens* (the typical form) is the predominant crop in Queensland and is the species botanist Ferdinand von Mueller found and described in the 1800s (it was one of 800 Australian species then unknown to science, that were recorded by von Mueller). The genus *Davidsonia* is named after John Ewen Davidson, who arrived in Cardwell with his business partner ED Thomas and set up a sugar-cane plantation in 1865. The most common Indigenous name is ooray (phonetically wirray in Ma:Mu and wiiraa in Nkdjonji),

and that is being resurrected. The first Ooray Plum Festival was held on the Johnstone River near Malanda on 28–29 September 2019.

NUTRITIONAL PROPERTIES

Both types of Davidson plums are an excellent source of potassium, vitamin E, lutein, zinc, folate, calcium and magnesium. Potassium is vital for the heartbeat, movement of the muscles, nerves and also kidney function. Zinc and vitamin E are needed for youthful and glowing skin. The plum also possesses anti-diabetic properties and has the ability to reduce obesity and lower hypertension.

AVAILABLE FORMS

Fresh, dried or frozen.

COOKING WITH DAVIDSON PLUMS

While you would never eat this incredibly sour fruit raw (although Paul van Reyk did, see pages 52–53), it will earn its place in your kitchen because of the wonderful sauces and jams it makes. It adds a beautiful fruity and earthy flavour, somewhat like beetroot.

To tame that sourness, rather than drowning the plums in sugar, try lemon juice, or pair them with apples or pears.

They work well with akudjura (dried bush tomatoes) and can be teamed with sweet chilli sauce for a marinade or dressing. A Davo plum dressing sauce or marinade works well with magpie goose, duck or 'roo. Chef Jean-Paul Bruneteau suggests using the juice as an alternative to vinegar for a tangy salad dressing. They can also flavour dairy products, such as yoghurt.

And do try the Brookie's Byron Slow Gin from Cape Byron Distillery, made from Davidson plums grown outside the distillery in a rainforest (see Sources and resources).

· ·

THREAT FROM ITS NAMESAKE

There is an irony in naming this fruit after the renowned sugar-cane grower JE Davidson. Because of land clearing for agricultural and urban development – sugar-cane farming being one major threat – all wild Davidson plums are now listed as an endangered and threatened species in New South Wales and are included in both the *Environment Protection and Biodiversity Conservation Act 1999* (Cth) and the *Threatened Species Conservation Act 1995* (NSW).

· ·

RAYMOND KERSH

TASMANIAN ATLANTIC SALMON FILLET WITH DAVIDSON PLUM VINAIGRETTE

Serves 2

A rich sweet and sour sauce works wonders with the salmon fillet. Keen cooks may seek out the pleasantly tangy fruit of the native tamarind, whose habitat is the south-east coast.

2 salmon fillets
fresh dill, to garnish

Vinaigrette
4 Davidson plums
2 tablespoons honey

2 teaspoons brown sugar
2 tablespoons tamarind
  concentrate
2 tablespoons macadamia oil or
  olive oil
1 red onion, finely chopped

1. For the vinaigrette, cut the plums in half and take out the seed. Spoon the ripe fruit out of the skin and mash it up in a mixing bowl. Add the remaining vinaigrette ingredients, except the red onion, and continue mashing. When sufficiently crushed, add the red onion.
2. Grill or pan-fry the salmon fillets in oil (preferably macadamia or olive) until medium or medium–rare.
3. Place the salmon fillets on serving plates and place some of the vinaigrette along the centre of the fillet. Sprinkle the fresh dill on top of the vinaigrette and serve.

PAUL VAN REYK

....

DAVIDSON PLUM JAM

Makes just under 2 kg of jam

With whooping excitement I came across a profusion of Davidson plums at the Mullumbimby Markets recently. I don't know what I expected but my first surprise was that they looked like – well, plums, coloured an ashy blue through to a bruise purple; and where I had been expecting something perhaps the size of a lilly pilly these were the size of ping pong balls. The next surprise was the taste, at the sour end of the scale on first bite but sweetening as the juice exuded. I could have eaten them fresh and been happy. But my inner bush homemaker would be satisfied by nothing less than jam. I found the simplest recipe I could and made up enough for three jars, to sufficient approbation from severe judges of jams. PVR

1 kg Davidson plums
1 kg sugar (use jam-setting sugar or caster sugar)
½ vanilla bean, split lengthways or 1½ teaspoons vanilla extract
juice of 1 small lemon

1. Cut the plums in half and remove the seeds but keep the skin on.
2. Put all the ingredients in a saucepan and mix well. Put the saucepan over high heat. Do not add any other liquid. The plums will soon begin to sweat their juice and this will combine with the sugar and create enough liquid.

3. When the mixture is boiling, reduce the heat and let the mixture simmer for 1 hour, stirring every 15 minutes or so just to keep the mix liquefying.
4. Meanwhile, preheat the oven to 250°C. Wash and clean the jars you are going to use for the jam and let them drain dry.
5. After an hour, test the jam for setting consistency. Put a small amount of the mixture on a plate. Put the plate in the fridge or a cool place for 2 or 3 minutes. Take the plate and tip it on its side. If the mixture doesn't run down the plate, the jam is set. If it does, keep simmering and test again in 5 minutes. Repeat until the jam is set.
6. Take the jam off the stove and set aside.
7. Put the glass jars – without their lids – in the oven and leave them there for 15 minutes to sterilise. Turn the oven off and transfer the jars to a surface that won't burn from the heat of the glass.
8. Spoon the jam into the jars, filling them to the top. Put the lids on tight. Leave the jam for at least a day before eating. This jam will be sharp in flavour and chunky as the skins have been left on. Store in the fridge, when opened, for up to two months.

Paul van Reyk is a friend and colleague, a talented, adventurous home and sometime professional cook and an inveterate jam maker. As he says: 'I've been an avid fan of eating native fruits since I first bit into a lilly pilly, that thumbnail-sized native relative of the jambu (aka water apple) a favourite fruit of my Sri Lankan childhood. I have a finger lime tree in my backyard that grudgingly gives me a dozen fruit each year. The Davidson plum has until now eluded me: I tried growing a tree myself once, but several months of drought did for it.'

RAYMOND KERSH

······································

BUSH FOOD FRUIT CRUMBLE

Serves 8–10

I love these Australian variations on old favourites, especially ones as easy as this to make. The Davos add tang to this much-loved dessert.

Crumble

295 g caster sugar

200 g salted butter

250 g plain flour

65 g rolled oats

65 g shredded coconut

2 teaspoons honey

2 teaspoons crushed wattleseeds

Poached fruit

1 kg sliced pears, or you can use apples or plums

8 Davidson plums, seeded

2 cups rosella buds

200 g granulated sugar

1 teaspoon vanilla extract

1. To make the crumble, mix together all the ingredients in a bowl, until you have a crumb-like texture. Set aside.
2. For the poached fruit, put all the ingredients in a saucepan and simmer until the pears are soft.
3. Preheat the oven to 200°C.
4. Half-fill eight to ten small ovenproof moulds, or one large ovenproof mould, with the poached fruit. Sprinkle the crumble mixture over generously.
5. Bake the moulds in the oven for 30 minutes, then serve hot.

ROSELLA BUDS

There are many native Australian hibiscus, from which we get the rosella bud, but those most widely used are *Hibiscus sabdariifolia* which grows wild in the Northern Territory or *H. heterophyllus*, an east coast native. The sour buds of the first are used for jam, and of *H. heterophyllus* in sweet dishes. The fibre was used by Indigenous Australians to spin string, and the young roots and leaves were also eaten.

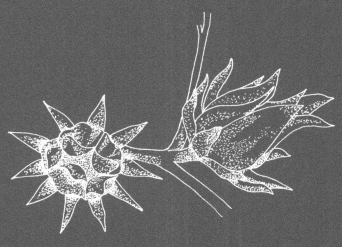

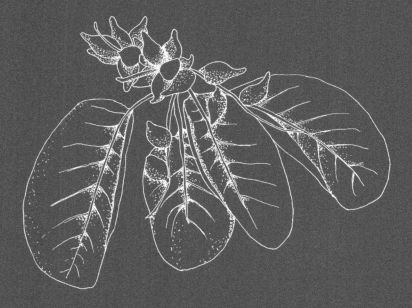

AUSTRALIAN FRUITING RAINFOREST PLANTS

Why does this country have so many fruiting rainforest plants – there are 2400 in north-east Australia alone – and why do their fruits have such high levels of nutrients? Those included in this book are Davidson plums, Illawarra plums, riberry and finger lime.

I asked Dr Maurizio Rossetto, the principal research scientist and manager of Evolutionary Ecology at the National Herbarium of New South Wales in Sydney about this. He told me that they are currently researching this at the Herbarium. He explained, 'A simple interpretation that is emerging from our work is that dispersal is one of the main factors impacting on the distribution and assembly of rainforest plants.' In other words, the expansion/contraction events that rainforest vegetation went through during geological times are likely to have favoured species that produce easy-to-disperse fruits – easy to disperse

in the sense that they are eaten by animals, then their seeds are excreted. These include a lot of fleshy-fruited species.

Many of these fruits are quite large, which means they were suited (in evolutionary terms) to larger animals. So one theory that Dr Rossetto and his colleagues are exploring is that Australian megafauna lasted longer than was previously thought. It seems the megafauna had a more important role in dispersing until relatively recent times. The team at the Herbarium is now also looking at how Aboriginal communites disperse some of these fruits.

This makes a lot of sense. Indigenous Kakadu plum (*Terminalia ferdinandiana*) harvesters today tell me that, like their ancestors, they always leave some pits in the ground as they pass through and harvest the fruit. But, as Dr Rossetto explained to me at the outset, the reasons for the extraordinary number of flowering fruit trees are complex.

FINGER LIME

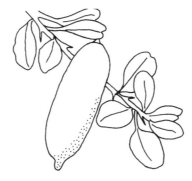

This Pliocene survivor – making it around 5 million years old – is undoubtedly the most popular of the Australian native fruits. *Citrus australasica* comes in many flesh colours, primarily pink, green, red and yellow. The little finger-shaped fruits, up to 10 centimetres long, are concealed in a prickly tree, and require careful picking due to the hard thorns. The edible flesh inside has small, sticky 'bubbly' globules, rather like tiny pearls or caviar.

Finger limes once grew in the wild, in tropical to subtropical rainforest, from the north-east coast of New South Wales to south-east Queensland, but now they are mainly cultivated. In its natural habitat finger limes fruit all year round with a burst from January to March. The Wiradjuri word for finger lime is 'Gulalung'.

In the early 19th century, finger lime plants were removed to make way for European agriculture but, luckily, some survived, and now they are being grown by producers and in home gardens all over Australia. They can be grown in the ground or in pots. I have a friend in Adelaide who raises a huge crop in her home garden every year.

They are also now appearing increasingly in greengrocers and even some supermarkets.

NUTRITIONAL PROPERTIES

The fruit is quite high in vitamin C, with the red variety having the richest quantity. There are also good levels of lutein, potassium and vitamin E.

AVAILABLE FORMS

Best bought and used fresh.

COOKING WITH FINGER LIMES

The tart and tangy flavour of finger limes varies from mild and 'limey' to pink grapefruit bitter, and you can enjoy it without elaborate cooking. Indeed, with finger limes fresh is best.

To prepare finger limes, simply cut them in half and squeeze out the pearls of fruit. There's no pith, segmentation or seeds – they're ready to go. Sprinkle them on fish, anyway you cook it, or oysters. They also make excellent marmalade and jams and complement melons and desserts. And – this idea took around 5 million years to perfect – add them to a gin and tonic or a vodka and tonic.

· ·

THE *CITRUS* GENUS: A TRIP THROUGH TIME

The genus *Citrus*, comprising some of the most widely cultivated fruit crops worldwide, includes an uncertain number of species. *Citrus* diversified during the late Miocene epoch from 23 million to around 5 million years ago through a rapid south-east Asian radiation (or warming of climate), which correlates with a marked weakening of the monsoons. A second radiation enabled by migration across the Wallace Line (the boundary that separates the ecozone of Asia and the Australasian ecozone) gave rise to the Australian limes in the early Pliocene epoch, around 5 million to 3 million years ago.

· ·

ANDREW FIELKE

OYSTER AND LEEK TARTLET WITH FINGER LIME CAVIAR BEURRE BLANC

Serves 4

This classic recipe, from one of Australia's most experienced bush food chefs, pitches the sweet tartness of finger limes against the sea flavour of oysters in a shortcrust pastry with crisp leeks.

3–4 finger limes
2 young leeks, washed and
    trimmed
vegetable oil, for deep-frying
50 g butter
white pepper, ground
16 oysters, shucked
4 x 6 cm sour cream or shortcrust
    pastry tart shells, pre–blind
    baked (these can be bought
    frozen at most supermarkets)
5–10 g salmon roe

Beurre blanc
juice of 2 lemons (approximately
    80 ml)
150 g cold unsalted butter, diced
sea salt
1–2 teaspoons sugar, as needed

FINGER LIME

1. To make the beurre blanc, reduce the lemon juice in a stainless steel saucepan over medium heat to about one-third of its original volume. Swirl in the butter cubes, a few at a time, until incorporated. Do not allow to boil. Season to taste with the sea salt and balance the acid with a little sugar.
2. Cut the finger limes in half crossways and squeeze out the flesh, removing the seeds, if any. This is the finger lime caviar.
3. Cut a 6 cm-long piece from the pale section of each leek and slice it lengthways into fine julienne.
4. Heat the oil in a saucepan or deep-fryer to 150°C, then fry the leek julienne until light golden brown and crisp. Transfer to a bowl lined with paper towel and set aside in a warm place.
5. Slice the remaining leek into thin rings, then place in a frying pan over medium–low heat and simmer gently in half the butter until tender. Season to taste with the white pepper.
6. In a separate frying pan, warm the oysters gently in the remaining butter – do not overcook.
7. Stir the finger lime caviar into the beurre blanc.
8. Place some warm stewed leek into each tartlet shell, followed by four warm oysters. Top the tartlets with the beurre blanc and the crisp leek. Garnish with the salmon roe and serve.

Tip: If you can, buy live oysters and shuck them yourself, add a little liquor from the oysters to the butter.

Andrew Fielke, with his Red Ochre restaurants, was one of the first non-Indigenous authorities on bush foods. Today, Andrew supplies products to food services, chefs and you. Find his website in Sources and resources. His book Australia's Creative Native Cuisine *was published in 2020.*

QUANDONG

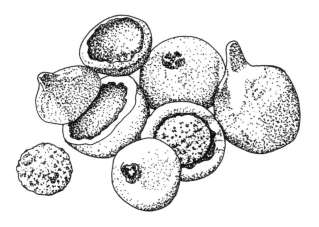

Also known as the desert peach, the vibrant red fruit of *Santalum acuminatum* – a species of sandalwood – has been a favourite of the Indigenous desert people for over 60 000 years and was taken up by the colonists in a big way.

S. acuminatum is a relatively small tree that grows to a height of 4 metres, with long olive-green leaves that hang from thin drooping stems. The fruit is the size of an Australian 20 cent coin and in shape resembles a fat avocado. The colour of its skin is a shiny red (occasionally yellow). Inside, as with an avocado, is a large stone encased in flesh. Although the stone is edible, it contains small quantities of toxins so it should be roasted before eating.

The kernels within the stone were crushed to make a paste, which was used by Aborigines to rub into the skin against aches and pains.

The stones were used by Indigenous children for games

and by women for making necklaces and other jewellery. The wood of the tree was used in carving and for making bowls and dishes. Later, non-Indigenous Australians used the stones and wood in the same way.

The fruit ripens in spring, changing from bright green to scarlet, so it has been likened to a Christmas tree hanging with baubles. It grows naturally from New South Wales' central west across to the Great Victoria Desert.

The most puzzling thing about this much-loved fruit is that it is not used more widely. It has been cultivated since at least 1875 (by John Ragless at Angmering Vale in Enfield South Australia). Home cooks and chefs have sung its praises for years. Yet it still does not appear in our greengrocers and fruit shops. I can only surmise this is because it needs to be cooked. But then why are there not more commercially made quandong jams and sauces?

NUTRITIONAL PROPERTIES

The fruit is high in vitamin C (twice that of an orange) and is a very good source of vitamin E, folate and magnesium. It is also a valuable vegetarian/vegan source of calcium, iron and zinc. It's also rich in immune system–boosting phenolic-based antioxidants, which reduce inflammation.

AVAILABLE FORMS

Fresh, dried or frozen.

COOKING WITH QUANDONG

Like most native Australian fruit, the quandong is acidic and tart, but with a background saltiness. It has been used by European cooks for well over 100 years. I first tasted the quandong cake made by Gayle Quarmby at Outback Pride, the Australian native nursery she and her husband Mike began at Reedy Creek in South Australia. You'll find the recipe on page 65.

Fresh quandongs need very little cooking and this should be done over a gentle heat. Dried quandongs, which is how they will often be purchased, should be rehydrated for a couple of hours in cold water. You can then use the water to cook them in.

Quandongs are most often used in making sweet dishes: cakes, tarts, pies, jams and sweet jellies. But they can also be used to make tart sauces to accompany kangaroo, lamb or sausages. This kind of sauce teams well with chilli.

· ·

THE EMU AND THE QUANDONG

There is a natural relationship between the emu and the quandong. The quandong plant is a root parasite, so it needs a host tree to provide its nutrients. Emus love quandongs and therefore spread the seeds far and wide. The seeds are fertilised by emu dung and, because emus shelter under shade trees, the seed will have a host plant. It's three-way cooperation.

· ·

GAYLE QUARMBY

....

MY ALL-TIME FAVOURITE QUANDONG CAKE

Serves 4–6

*I was served this cake when I visited Reedy Creek and ate far
too many slices. Gayle says you can replace the quandongs with
muntries (native apples, see page 105) if they're unavailable
or out of season.*

250 ml cream
2 eggs, beaten
225 g self-raising flour
pinch of salt

220 g caster sugar
50 g rehydrated dried, or fresh/
    frozen dried quandong halves
cream or ice cream, to serve

1. Preheat the oven to 180°C. Grease then line a 23 cm cake tin with baking paper.
2. Using an electric mixer, whip the cream until peaks form. Add the beaten eggs and mix to incorporate. Add the flour, salt and sugar to the mixer and mix until everything is fully combined.
3. Fill a cake tin with the batter, then arrange the quandong halves over the surface.
4. Bake in the oven for about 1 hour until the cake smells yummy and cooked.
5. Serve the cake warm with a dollop of cream or ice cream.

*Gayle Quarmby is one half of the team (with husband, Michael) that started the
Outback Pride Fresh nursery at Reedy Creek in South Australia. Gayle grew up
with the Arrernte people and gathered bush foods with the locals as a child.
Find Gayle and Michael's current project in Sources and resources.*

BRET CAMERON

SEARED KANGAROO LOIN, WATTLESEED, BROWN RICE, QUANDONG AND WARRIGAL GREENS

Serves 4

I urge you, when searing 'roo, heat your pan (preferably a heavy black or cast iron) to extremely hot for a quick one-minute-each-side sear. And again, the native fruit is a perfect match for the 'roo.

pinch of salt

200 g brown rice

10 g ground wattleseeds

50 g butter, cut into small dice

600 g kangaroo loin

1 tablespoon extra virgin olive oil

100 g warrigal greens

Quandongs

200 ml water

100 ml white wine vinegar

2 aniseed myrtle leaves

50 g raw sugar

pinch of salt

30 g dried quandong halves

1. For the quandongs, bring the water, vinegar, aniseed myrtle leaves, sugar and salt to the boil. Turn off the heat and leave the mixture for 10 minutes to infuse.
2. Pour the liquid over the quandongs in a bowl, then leave for 3 hours to rehydrate the fruit.
3. Preheat the oven to 130°C.
4. Bring a large saucepan of salted water to the boil, then pour in the rice. Bring back to the boil, then reduce the heat and simmer for 15 minutes. Drain the rice into a colander.
5. Spread the rice evenly over a baking tray lined with baking paper. Evenly sprinkle over the ground wattleseeds and cubes of butter, then gently toss with a fork.
6. Bake in the oven for 15 minutes, tossing the rice with a fork every 5 minutes. When done, the rice should be evenly toasted

and have a nutty aroma. Set aside and keep warm.

7. Trim any sinew off the kangaroo and cut into four even pieces.

8. Heat a medium frying pan over high heat, add the olive oil and sear the kangaroo on each side for about 1 minute, until it is rare and you get a good caramelisation. It's important not to overcook the meat or it will become tough and dry. If you are not confident, use a thermometer and take the internal temperature to 50°C. When cooked, rest the meat for 5 minutes.

9. While the meat is resting, in the same pan sauté the warrigal greens for 30 seconds until wilted. Drain.

10. To serve, divide the warm rice between four plates. Slice each piece of kangaroo into three and place the meat beside the rice. Drain the quandongs and divide evenly between the plates. (You can use some of the pickling liquid as a sauce too.) Gently lay the warrigal greens around the plates and serve.

Bret Cameron is a passionate voice for bush foods. Head chef at The Pacific Club Bondi Beach, his style of cooking brings these ingredients to the table in an approachable way, underpinned by locally sourced, sustainable produce.

. . . .

ANISEED / ANISE MYRTLE

The leaf of a rainforest tree (*Syzygium anisatum*), now quite rare in the wild, was once native to a handful of areas in north-east New South Wales, primarily the Bellingen and Nambucca valleys.

The leaf is sweet and cooling on the palate with aromas of menthol and aniseed. It is high in antioxidants, vitamin E, lutein, magnesium and phenolics and can be used for flavouring desserts, sweet sauces and preserves and in savoury sauces and marinades.

It was traditionally used for weight loss, to promote lactation and to ease stomach complaints.

. . . .

REBECCA SULLIVAN

QUANDONG AND FINGER LIME PRAWN COCKTAIL

Serves 4 as a starter

Another Australian take on a classic (from the 1970s). This one has a delicious tart flavour that would have rocked them back then: it used to be served before Steak Diane. Maybe try a 'roo Diane? I'll work on it.

1 baby cos lettuce, washed, dried
and pulled into leaves
1 mini radicchio, washed, dried and
pulled into leaves
500–600 g cooked prawns, peeled
with tails left intact
pinch of akudjura (dried and
powdered bush tomato),
to garnish
1 small handful of chives, chopped,
to garnish

Sauce
4 tablespoons aïoli
2 tablespoons quandong chutney
(see opposite)
3 teaspoons Worcester sauce
Tabasco sauce, to taste
2 teaspoons creamy horseradish
squeeze of lemon juice
caviar from 2 finger limes
salt
ground Tasmanian pepperberry,
to taste

1. Make the sauce by combining the aïoli, chutney, Worcester, Tabasco, horseradish, lemon juice and finger lime in a medium bowl. Taste and season with salt and Tasmanian pepperberry to your liking.
2. Layer the cos and radicchio leaves in four serving glasses or bowls.
3. Holding the shell of the prawns' tails, dip the prawns into the sauce and heavily coat them. Place the prawns on top of your lettuce garnish.
4. Sprinkle the akudjura and chives over the prawns to garnish. Place in the fridge until ready to serve.

NEVILLE BONNEY

....

QUANDONG FRUIT CHUTNEY

Makes about 800 g

Use this chutney in the sauce for the preceding recipe.

2½ cups quandongs, fresh or dried
2 cups sugar
water to cover
1 tablespoon sultanas
1 dessertspoon mixed fruit
½ an apple
pinch of salt
pinch of ground cloves
pinch of pepper
1 teaspoon lemon juice

1. Boil the quandongs until tender, add the sugar and simmer for
    30 minutes
2. Add all the other ingredients, simmer for further 30 minutes.
3. Pour into sterilised glass jars, seal with the lids and store.

Neville Bonney is the author of Jewel of the Australian Desert, *a book dedicated
to the history and botany of the quandong, with a number of recipes (see
Bibliography for details).*

FORAGING, DOS AND DON'TS

Here is a cautionary tale from veteran forager Vic Cherikoff. In his book *Wild Foods*, he writes of having foraged the delicious finger cherry (*Rhodomyrtus macrocarpa*) from rainforests south of Cairns. The problem is that this fruit can harbour a fungus, which can render anyone eating it blind. Some plants do have the fungus, some don't. And you can't tell by looking so, as Vic says, the risk of blindness is so high he doesn't even recommend a taste.

That's an extreme example, but it should be remembered that there are many poisonous wild plants out there. But poisoning is not the only problem with foraging. This is what Mike Quarmby, the pioneer bush foods horticulturist who initiated the Outback Pride nursery in South Australia had to say: 'Foraging or picking Australian native plants from the wild is breaking the law. If you take plants out of the bush, you're depleting the seed source and the natural regeneration of those things.'

It almost seems like sacrilege to say this, in an era when the bush is crawling with chefs foraging for fodder. But Mike is right – foraging is illegal unless you have a picker licence which, in New South Wales for instance, includes restrictions such as only being able to pick certain species of plants.

It's one thing for Indigenous people with a deep understanding of what they're doing to pick plants for their own use. It's quite another for people to forage without understanding the potential problems of pulling up anything they see. It's possible they may take a unique and irreplaceable specimen from the wild.

When the Quarmbys go out to select plants to breed, they're accompanied by local Indigenous people, who help them select the best specimens and those that are not in short supply.

If you don't have Indigenous elders to take you out foraging, what's the next best thing? There are more and more tours being organised by Indigenous groups to show non-Indigenous people the right way to forage, and what to forage. See Sources and resources.

FORAGING FOR PAPERBARK

One piece of practical advice if you're foraging for paperbark (especially in the city). Firstly, choose from high on the tree (higher than a tall dog can lift its leg!). Secondly, the inner bark is softer and better for wrapping and cooking.

RIBERRY

Some call the fruit of the lilly pilly tree a riberry, others just call them a lilly pilly. I'm sticking with riberry. Having cleared that up, there are about sixty lilly pillies in Australia, most in the genus *Syzygium*, and most have edible fruit, although some have fruit that is overly astringent or bland. The one we will concentrate on is *Syzygium luehmannii*, small-leaved or clove lilly pilly, but I'll also recommend *S. paniculatum*, magenta lilly pilly.

The fruit of *S. luehmannii* (from now on I will just refer to it as riberry) is small – up to 13 millimetres long, pear-shaped and dull red, with one pip. The tree with its tear-shaped leaves can grow up to 30 metres in the wild, but in cultivation and as an ornamental street tree it is kept to between 5 and 10 metres. It fruits from December to February.

S. luehmannii trees are generally found in the wild in northern New South Wales and are also native to rainforests from Kempsey, New South Wales, to Cooktown in north-east Queensland. The species also has the potential to be grown in many other areas.

The riberry is the only bush food you are likely to find growing on street trees and, if you live in Sydney, keep your eyes open for them. Polish-born scientist and researcher into the properties of Australian bush foods, Dr Izabela Konczak recalls finding them growing in front of the CSIRO building where she worked.

The magenta lilly pilly (*S. paniculatum*) is a small- to medium-sized rainforest tree that grows to 8 metres. It produces white flower-clusters at the end of each branch between November and February. The deep magenta fruits, which may be spherical or egg-shaped, mature in May and are larger and sweeter than those of

S. luehmannii but without as much clove accent.

The magenta lilly pilly is found only in New South Wales, in a narrow, linear coastal strip from Upper Lansdowne, south-west of Port Macquarie, to Conjola National Park on the mid south coast. While the fruit from this tree is large and sweet, it is an intermittent fruiter.

I have two lilly pillies in my little courtyard in inner Sydney, which I bought before becoming aware of the differences between species. One is *S. luehmannii*, and fruits prolifically, the other I can't identify but it bears no fruit. If you do want to grow your own, make sure you get either or both of the good ones that I recommend here.

NUTRITIONAL PROPERTIES

It is estimated that 100 grams of riberries contain 50 per cent of the recommended daily intake of folate, they're high in antioxidants and magnesium, and have useful levels of calcium, vitamin E and manganese.

AVAILABLE FORMS
Fresh or dried.

COOKING WITH RIBERRY
Having had my own fruit to play with, I've got to know this one quite well. The fruit is refreshingly tart, with a spicy sweet flavour, with musky notes and a hint of clove, cinnamon and nutmeg often present. It makes beautiful jams, relishes and sorbets, and works in salads and desserts, as well as sauces to accompany game meats, especially duck, and poultry, pork and lamb. It can even be used as you would a juniper berry (there is a riberry gin available).

When you are cooking with an astringent fruit like the riberry, bush foods expert Vic Cherikoff cautions to avoid pairing it with astringent fruits like cherry and apple, but rather combine with lemon and lime.

. . . .

COUSIN CLOVE

Riberry's cousin, the clove, is also from the genus *Syzygium* (species *aromaticum*). Cloves are actually the dried, unopened flower buds of the tree. When you cook with riberries, add a tiny amount of clove to accentuate the clove notes in the riberry.

. . . .

COOKING ACCIDENT

Jean-Paul Bruneteau was distracted by a phone call while he was cooking up a big batch of riberries. After 45 minutes, he writes 'the liquor had almost evaporated but, amazingly, the fruit had not collapsed'. After cooling it overnight, it had kept its full flavour.

. . . .

JUDE MAYALL

....

BANANA RIBERRY BREAD

Makes 1 loaf

Jude's experiments with our bush food gems, like this variation on good old banana bread, make a lot of sense and add another dimension. And like all of her recipes, it's simplicity itself.

100 g butter
220 g caster sugar
3 ripe bananas, mashed
2 eggs
½ teaspoon vanilla extract

225 g plain flour
1 teaspoon bicarbonate of soda
½ teaspoon salt
½ cup riberries

1. Preheat the oven to 175°C.
2. Using an electric mixer, cream the butter and sugar until pale.
3. Add the mashed bananas, the eggs then the vanilla and process until blended.
4. Sift the plain flour, bicarb soda and salt together. Gently stir the banana mixture and the riberries into the dry ingredients.
5. Pour into a greased loaf tin that has been lined with baking paper
6. Bake for approximately 1 hour. Because oven temperatures can vary, prick the bread with a skewer and, when it comes out clean, it's cooked. Store in the fridge.

Jude Mayall has been the OutbackChef since 2005. OutbackChef works directly with wild-harvesters, Indigenous communities, farmers and growers in regional and remote areas. You'll find Jude's website listed in Sources and resources.

RAYMOND KERSH

....

RIBERRY SALSA

Makes 1 jar

Serve this riberry salsa with any type of fish,
beef, kangaroo or wallaby. RK

¼ cup riberries, halved or quartered if large
2 roma tomatoes
1 small red onion, finely chopped
extra virgin olive oil or macadamia oil
half a bunch of native Australian or Vietnamese mint

1. Place the riberries in a bowl.
2. Chop the roma tomatoes into small chunks, discarding the pulp, and add to the riberries in the bowl, along with the onion.
3. Drizzle over the extra virgin olive oil or macadamia oil, gently toss with the mint, then it's ready to serve. Store, as usual, in sterilised glass jars in the fridge.

NATIVE BUSH MINT/RIVER MINT

There are about ninety species of native bush mint that are
endemic to Australia. One particular plant is round-leaf mint bush
(*Prostanthera rotundifolia*). Coming into spring, it puts on a beautiful
spread of light-coloured flowers. Traditionally it was used as a
medicinal herb – for headaches and colds. These days it's more of
a culinary herb. Another, river mint *(Mentha australis)*, is summer
growing, thriving along riverbanks after flood, particularly in the
Murray–Darling Basin waterways. It was enthusiastically embraced
by the early settlers and used with their roast lamb. It makes an
interesting mint tea, which is reputedly good for easing the effects
of colds. The crushed leaves were sniffed to relieve headache.

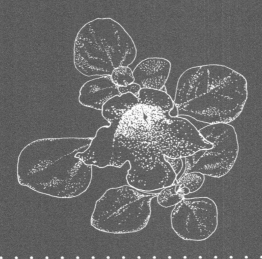

JOHN NEWTON

....

RIBERRY RELISH

Makes 400 g, 1 jar

I made this relish using Syzygium leuhmannii *fruit from my
own courtyard tree, which I first served with slow-cooked duck
marylands. It would work with any grilled or roasted meat, or even
as a sauce over ice cream.*

60 g brown sugar
2 cups riberries
zest and juice of 1 large lemon or 2 limes
2 thyme sprigs (remove after cooking)

1. In a non-reactive saucepan over medium heat, add all the relish
    ingredients and stir to combine.
2. Allow to simmer, with the lid on, stirring occasionally until the mixture
    coalesces for 30 minutes, or more. Taste to confirm. Remove from
    the heat, allow to cool then serve. Store any remaining relish in a
    sterilised glass jar in the fridge.

BUSH FOODS AS MEDICINE

As it was with food, Indigenous medicine was ignored by Europeans for over 200 years. As science is discovering, after tens of thousands of years living in the same place and learning from the plant life around them, Indigenous knowledge was vast. There are, however, obstacles to a complete understanding of Indigenous medicine.

First and foremost, Indigenous healers used a combination of plants and ritual, weaving together the material and the spiritual. In our non-Indigenous search for what does and doesn't work in terms of Western scientific method, we can only examine and validate one side of this: the material.

One example of Western scientific testing of a traditional plant used in bush medicine was the examination of the medicinal potential of *Scaevola spinescens* (currant bush, maroon bush). Its toxicity, antibacterial and antiviral activities were examined at Griffith University. The report states that, 'Accounts exist of aqueous extracts of *S. spinescens* root bark being used to cure cancer, although their efficacy is yet to be verified in controlled lab studies.' By accounts, the researchers mean anecdotal evidence. And what was their conclusion after putting this plant through their rigorous testing?

'In conclusion' they wrote, 'the results of this study partially validate the traditional Aboriginal usage of *S. spinescens* to treat bacterial and viral diseases and indicate that *S. spinescens* is worthy of further study.' Those interested in reading the complete study should see the Bibliography.

S. spinescens has been studied for many years, there's even a book: *Nature's Helping Hand: Scaevola spinescens, History and Use in Western Australia:*

The Maroon Bush Story. There is a link to this book in the Bibliography.

Below I've listed four of the more widely used Indigenous medicine plants (and one grub):

Beach bean. This purple-flowering plant (*Canavalia rosea*) is found on beaches and dunes. A carefully prepared extract from the roots is rubbed on the skin to relieve aches and pains.

Gumbi gumbi. A small shrub with little star-shaped yellow flowers and yellow/orange-skinned fruit, gumbi gumbi (*Pittosporum angustifolium*) is found throughout the drier areas of Australia and is perhaps the most potent, yet versatile, Indigenous medicine.

Research published in *Pharmacognosy Communications* (October 2011) into the benefits of gumbi gumbi found that it had an array of benefits including being an anti-pruritic, anti-viral, detoxifier, blood pressure regulator and immune system booster. (Pharmacognosy is defined as the branch of knowledge concerned with medicinal drugs obtained from plants or other natural sources.) The fruit and seeds are known for their medicinal properties, but it's the leaves used as a tea, a tonic, dried in capsules or in salves/creams that are most effective.

Lemon grasses. The leaves, stems and roots of native lemon grasses (*Cymbopogon ambiguus* A. Camus) are liquefied and taken orally to treat coughs and diarrhoea. The root can also be applied to the ears as a poultice for earaches.

Dr Darren Grice at Griffith University, says a molecule called eugenol is present in the plant, which is used for treating headaches, colds and muscle pain, and that it has the same therapeutic benefits as aspirin.

These grasses grow around drier parts of the country and are identified by green

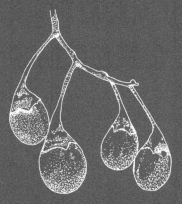

tufts at the end of thin stalks, which give a citrus scent when crushed.

Kangaroo apple. Both *Solanum laciniatum* and *S. aviculare* are natural anti-inflammatory steroids that aid in the production of cortisone. They're useful for treating aching joints and wounds and will encourage skin regrowth over scars. As a poultice, the kangaroo apple has been used for these purposes for thousands of years.

The orange fruits are good to eat but only when ripe: the unripe fruit and leaves are poisonous.

Witchetty grubs. Crushed and made into a paste, these grubs are used to help heal skin. They are an example of a resource with more than one use – nutrition and medicine.

WARRIGAL GREENS

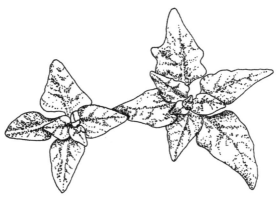

Warrigal greens, or New Zealand spinach (*Tetragonia tetragonioides*), was the first Australian bush food plant to become a staple in France, finding its way there via Joseph Banks. (The plant was originally named *T. cornuta* by Banks – cornuta meaning crescent-shaped.) *T. tetragonioides* is a low-lying, flowering plant, a succulent, which grows well in saline soil and around sandy shorelines.

It will form a dense carpet of thick heart-shaped leaves with yellow flowers and small hard fruit covered in horns.

The plant is native to eastern Asia, Australia and New Zealand and has been introduced to parts of Africa, Europe, North America and South America.

It is cultivated for its edible leaves, which have a similar flavour and texture to spinach. And, like spinach, it contains oxalates, which need to be removed by blanching then refreshing in cold water before cooking. For this reason, it was rarely eaten by Indigenous Australians.

If you live near the sea or a harbour, keep your eyes open for warrigal greens growing around you. There are several patches around the foreshore in Sydney where I live. If gathering from the urban wild (see Foraging, dos and don'ts, pages 70–71), wash the leaves thoroughly before you blanch them, in case dogs or herbicides have been around.

If you develop a taste for this native green, consider growing them at home. They grow profusely and their groundcover doesn't let weeds in. They like shade.

NUTRITIONAL PROPERTIES

They are naturally very high in antioxidants – James Cook took them on voyages to prevent scurvy among his crew. They're also high in fibre.

AVAILABLE FORMS

Best eaten fresh, after blanching. Do wash before eating.

COOKING WITH WARRIGAL GREENS

The taste of warrigal greens begins with a grassy or green bean flavour, which then develops a mild bitterness as you chew, which can be interesting in combination with other foods. Use them as you would spinach as a side green, especially with fish, and even in quiches. Or try them in stir-fries, where they stand up to heat much better than English spinach.

EMIGRATION TO FRANCE

The greens are naturally very high in antioxidants and James Cook took them on board the *Endeavour* to help prevent scurvy. Botanist Joseph Banks took *Tetragonia* seeds back to Kew Gardens from where they made their way to France. When contemporary Australian bush foods chef Jean-Paul Bruneteau returned to his native France after leaving at the age of twelve, he was astonished and delighted to find what he knew as warrigal greens growing in his uncle's garden in the south of France, as 'tetragon'.

SIMON BRYANT

WARRIGAL GREENS AND DESERT LIME PESTO WITH WHOLEMEAL PASTA

Serves 4

A zingier version of an Italian classic with a cunning collaboration between three native Australian foods. And it's remarkably easy to rustle up. Bewdy bellissimo pesto.

500 g wholemeal or spelt pasta
extra virgin olive oil, for drizzling
freshly ground black pepper
shaved parmesan cheese, to serve

Pesto and salad
250 g warrigal greens, baby
    leaves reserved for salad
1 large handful of sea parsley
    leaves and stalks, a few leaves
    reserved for salad

juice of 3 lemons
250 ml extra virgin olive oil, plus
    extra to cover jars and to
    drizzle over salad
200 g macadamia nuts
about 30 desert limes, plus a few
    halved limes for salad
4 garlic cloves, peeled
salt flakes
freshly ground black pepper
60 g parmesan cheese, grated

Continued over the page ➜

COOKING WITH THE OLDEST FOODS ON EARTH

1. To make the pesto, first blanch the warrigal greens in a large saucepan of boiling water for 1 minute, then rinse them in cold water. Drain well and squeeze out any excess liquid.
2. Roughly chop the blanched greens and sea parsley and place them in a food processor with the lemon juice and a little olive oil. Blend until the greens are roughly puréed. Add the macadamia nuts, desert limes and garlic and continue to blend until the mixture looks like crunchy peanut butter.
3. Continue blending slowly while drizzling in the remaining olive oil until you have a coarse pesto, then season to taste with salt and pepper. Add the parmesan and pulse to blend through, then check the seasoning.
4. Transfer the pesto to sterilised jars. Let it settle to remove any air bubbles, then cover with olive oil. This makes about 750 g of pesto. Store it in the fridge for up to 3 months. If you want to eat the pesto as a dip, add a little more oil to thin it down.
5. Cook the pasta in boiling salted water until *al dente*, then toss it in a little olive oil to prevent it from clumping together. Fold in 100 g of pesto per serving, drizzle with olive oil and season with black pepper.
6. Make a salad of the reserved warrigal greens baby leaves, sea parsley and desert limes. Season with salt to taste, then add a little olive oil and pepper.
7. Divide the pesto-coated pasta among bowls and garnish with the salad. Serve with shaved parmesan and a small bowl of extra pesto to the side, if you like.

Note: Simon advises: 'Sea parsley is a bit like parsley on steroids. (You can substitute dark green, hardy flat-leaf parsley, but you will need to use double the quantity.) Desert limes are punchier and sourer than regular Tahitians, so my substitute would be a small preserved lemon.'

Simon Bryant worked in The Grange kitchen in the Adelaide Hilton with Cheong Liew, was the co-host with Maggie Beer of ABC TV show The Cook and the Chef and is the Patron of Tasting Australia. This recipe is from his 2012 book, Simon Bryant's Vegies.

• •

DESERT LIME

A small round green fruit with green and yellow spots, the flesh inside has the same spots with a bubble-like appearance. As you'd expect from its name, it is drought-resistant and can continue to thrive in temperatures higher than 45°C and is equally tolerant of low temperatures. Its flavour is tart, astringent and bitter – way more intense than the Tahitian lime. Use in marmalades and refreshing drinks. The peel can be candied, so needn't be discarded when used. They freeze well. They're high in vitamins C (exceptionally high) and E, calcium, potassium, folate and lutein.

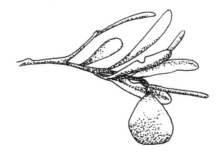

• •

MINDY WOODS

CREAMY SCRAMBLED EGGS WITH WARRIGAL GREENS

Serves 1

Great scrambled eggs take all of 60 seconds, should be just cooked, soft, fluffy and creamy. The addition of warrigal greens complements scrambled eggs beautifully and is far more flavourful than your standard English spinach. MW

(This recipe calls for fresh-picked Warrigal greens, best grow your own, they're easy JN.)

3 eggs
½ tablespoon butter
1½ tablespoons (or ½ egg shell) cream
1 small handful of fresh warrigal greens
Sea salt and freshly ground Dorrigo pepper, to taste
freshly toasted sourdough with lashings of cultured butter, to serve

1.   Whisk the eggs and cream together, to incorporate.
2.   Pick the warrigal green leaves and set aside.
3.   Melt the butter in a non-stick frying pan over medium–high heat.
4.   When the butter begins to bubble, add the warrigal green and sauté until slightly wilted. Season with salt and pepper.

4. Bring the pan back to medium–high heat and pour in the egg mixture. Allow the mix to sit for 5 seconds on the base of the pan so it just starts to set.
5. Run a rubber spatula around the very outside of the pan to bring the mixture from the outside toward the centre in long gentle strokes. This technique pushes the cooked egg off the base and piles it up into the centre, creating beautiful soft curds. Tilt the pan to run the uncooked mixture around the base of the hot pan and repeat until the mixture is just cooked through. This should only take 60 seconds or until the raw runny egg no longer spreads out onto the pan and you have a pile of soft, custardy egg, ever so slightly underdone.
6. Remove from the stove, slide onto your freshly cooked toast and enjoy.

Mindy Woods is a proud Bundjalung woman who owns and cooks at Karkalla Byron Bay. At Karkalla, Mindy shares her love of food, heritage and culture and is passionate about celebrating and protecting Australian bush foods.

SALTBUSHES

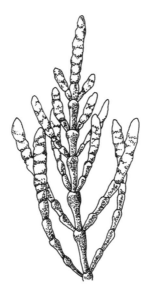

Saltbushes are halophytes, which are plants that adapt to saline soils. Although too much salt kills plants, halophytes deal with it by excreting excess salt or by absorbing a lot of water to keep a viable balance – the latter method is the tactic used by succulents. Saltbush habitats are beaches, seaside sand dunes, inland saltbush plains and salt marshes.

The first plant we think of when we use the term 'saltbush' is old man saltbush (*Atriplex nummularia*), a familiar sight in dry inland Australia, loved by sheep. It's a sprawling grey-blue shrub, which can grow to 3 metres and spread to 5 metres. There are about sixty varieties of this kind of saltbush spread across inland Australia. I recall seeing at least a dozen on a sheep property I visited outside Nyngan, in central New South Wales.

Other edible saltbushes are the coastal plants samphire (*Salicornia australis*), sea blite (*Suaeda australis*) and karkalla (*Carpobrotus rossii*) also known as native pigface. *C. rossii* is found in New South Wales but there are other varieties elsewhere.

Samphire grows mainly in extensive mats on coastal mudflats; sea blite on salt flats, inland saltpans and on sandbanks behind mangroves; and karkalla can be seen on beaches, coastal dunes and headlands.

Saltbush leaves contain natural mineral salts, calcium and protein, but research by the CSIRO shows that saltbush is extremely high in vitamin E. And it is good for both humans and for the sheep grazing on it – an extra reason to seek out saltbush lamb.

NUTRITIONAL PROPERTIES

Samphire has good levels of essential minerals including magnesium, potassium, calcium and sodium (quite a lot of sodium, in fact). That is in addition to a healthy amount of dietary fibre and vitamins A, B and C. It also contains unique compounds called fucoidans, often found in sea vegetables, which can have anti-inflammatory and antioxidant effects.

I'm not sure there is much nutritive value in either sea blite or karkalla (although as a sea plant, sea blite has high levels of iodine) but the leaves of karkalla can be used like aloe vera to treat stings and burns.

AVAILABLE FORMS

Old man saltbush fresh and dried, karkalla fresh.

COOKING WITH SALTBUSHES

Old man saltbush on the branch is delicious if simply thrown in a very hot pan with a little oil (macadamia is best) and flash-fried until crisp. The leaves on the branch can also be used as a bed for grilling meats or vegetables. Dried saltbush flakes can be added to bread, pasta and dukkah. Fresh or blanched they can be wrapped around fish or meat when grilling or roasting.

The Australian samphire, like the European version, is usually pickled, but in its guise as sea asparagus can be steamed, stir-fried or blanched and served with fish. Sea blite can be treated in the same way as samphire. Both work well when deep-fried as a salty side dish with fish.

Every part of the karkalla plant is edible and can also be eaten raw in salads, or cooked. The red fruit can be eaten either peeled or unpeeled and has been described by chef Matt Fleischmann as 'somewhere between a kiwifruit and a strawberry and maybe a fig, with a good whack of salt'. And there they are, just lying around our beaches, ripe for the picking (see Foraging dos and don'ts, pages 70–71).

The leaves of old man saltbush can be barbecued on skewers with prawns, scallops or fish, used in stir-fries, fried and eaten as a side to vegetables or meat, or cooked in omelettes with ham and cheese.

• •

CURE FOR STOMACH DISORDERS

Samphire is known for its digestive and anti-flatulence properties. Nicholas Culpeper, the 17th-century British herbalist, wrote of samphire (the European variety, but the same plant) that it was useful in curing ailments relating to 'ill digestions and obstructions', while being 'very pleasant to taste and stomach'. Is this true? Over to you …

• •

JOHN NEWTON

SAMPHIRE WITH MACADAMIA OIL AND FINGER LIME

Serves 4

Here is a recipe I adapted and rendered truly Australian with the addition of macadamia oil and finger limes.

1 bunch of samphire
macadamia or olive oil, to taste
2 finger limes
freshly ground black pepper, to taste

1. Pick over the samphire and make sure all the pieces are firm and crunchy. Remove any soft ends.
2. Cut the finger limes in half and squeeze out the caviar.
3. Blanch the samphire in boiling water for 1–2 minutes – the less time you leave it in the water, the crunchier it will be.
4. Drain the samphire and toss with the macadamia oil and pepper. Sprinkle with the finger lime caviar. Serve warm or cool with grilled or fried fish.

DAN CHURCHILL

··

BUTTERFLIED SALTBUSH CHOOK WITH CHARRED VEG

Serves 4

What I love about this dish is the addition of old man saltbush to an old family favourite. Who doesn't love a barbecued chook?

¼ cup dried saltbush (or bay leaves)

2 teaspoons ground cumin

1 teaspoon garlic powder

1 teaspoon cayenne pepper

2 teaspoons dried thyme

2 tablespoons lemon juice

90 ml olive oil

salt and pepper, to taste

1 whole chicken (about 1.8 kg), butterflied

2 red onions, quartered, with root end on

2 eggplants, sliced 5 mm thick lengthways

4 zucchini, sliced 5 mm thick lengthways

1. You can start this recipe the night before. Use a mortar and pestle or spice grinder to grind up the saltbush or bay leaves. Combine in a bowl with the cumin, garlic powder, cayenne pepper, thyme, 1 tablespoon of the lemon juice and half the olive oil. Season with salt and pepper.
2. Rub the marinade all over the chicken on both sides, getting into all the hidden joints. Marinate in the fridge for a minimum of 30 minutes, or overnight.
3. Bring the chicken to room temperature for 20 minutes, then preheat a covered barbecue grill plate to medium–high.

4. Put the chicken on the grill, skin side down. Close the barbecue lid (or cover with a large upside-down saucepan). Cook for about 8 minutes or until the skin is golden.
5. Turn the chicken over, cover again and cook for a further 15–20 minutes until the juices run clear when you pierce the thigh with a skewer. Transfer to a tray, cover with foil and set aside to rest.
6. Brush the vegetables with the remaining oil.
7. Start cooking the onions (they take the longest) on the barbecue for 5 minutes or until charred on both sides. Add the eggplant and zucchini and cook for 2–4 minutes until charred. Season the vegies with salt and pepper and pour the remaining lemon juice over them.
8. Serve the vegetables with the chook.

Dan Churchill is a self-trained chef whose first book Dude Food *was originally self-published. He's another graduate from the* MasterChef *school, and is now up to his fourth book. This recipe is from the 2016 book* Surfing the Menu *by Dan Churchill and Hayden Quinn.*

REBECCA SULLIVAN

....

SALTBUSH AND PEPPERBERRY BROTH

Makes 3 litres

*Another recipe from the team at Warndu. It's a rich
and versatile broth that can be drunk as a winter warmer
or used as a stock for casseroles or braises.*

1 kg bones (chicken, beef or pork)
2 chicken feet or pig's trotters for
    gelatine (optional)
4 litres filtered water
160 ml raw apple cider vinegar
1 brown onion
2 carrots
2 celery stalks

1 tablespoon dried Tasmanian
    pepperberries
1 small handful of saltbush leaves
2 coastal rosemary sprigs (see box)
    or use European rosemary
1 bunch of sea parsley
2 garlic cloves
salt and pepper, to taste

1. Put the bones, and feet or trotters, if using, into a large (5 litre)
    stockpot and add the filtered water. Add the vinegar and let it sit
    in the water for 30 minutes as the acid helps to make the nutrients
    more available.
2. Roughly chop the vegetables and add them to the water, along with
    the pepperberries, saltbush and rosemary and any other spices you
    may wish to add – but don't add the parsley or garlic yet.
3. Bring the broth to the boil. Once it has reached a vigorous boil,
    reduce to the lowest heat and simmer until done – for beef or pork
    broth 4–8 hours; for chicken broth 2–4 hours. For the first half hour

you will need to skim the scum from the surface of the stock. After that, there's no need to do anything until the last half hour, which is when you add the parsley and garlic. Check the seasoning.

4. Once cooked, sieve and store in a glass jar in the fridge for up to 5 days or freeze.

· ·

SEA PARSLEY

Sea parsley or sea celery (*Apium prostratum*) grows all along the southern coastline, but its leaf form and size vary considerably depending on where it grows. It looks like a shiny green parsley and is related to the European variety, but this version grows right on the coastline and is often submerged by incoming tides. It's this connection with the sea and surrounding vegetation that gives it its special flavour. Use it in soups, dressings, salads and with seafood and in white sauce.

COASTAL ROSEMARY

Westringia fruticosa is more often grown as a hedge or decorative garden plant but it still has a rosemary flavour and can be used as you would European rosemary.

· ·

FISH AND SEAFOOD

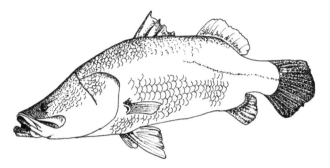

It was a great consolation to the colonists on the First Fleet to find an abundance of familiar and unfamiliar fish in Australia. First Fleet diarist Watkin Tench wrote, 'I shall not pretend to enumerate the variety of fish which are found' and then attempted to do so, before adding 'many of which are extremely delicious and many highly beautiful'. He nominates the snapper as the best eating.

There is a wealth of fish and seafood in Australian waters. You'll probably know most of them, but there are a few unusual ones. For example the cherubim (or cherabin, cherabun), *Macrobrachium rosenbergii*, is one of a number of freshwater prawns occurring in far northern Australia. You'll recognise it by its two large claws. I also have to mention our native oysters – the Sydney rock and the difficult-to-find, delicious and meaty *Ostrea angasi*, the Australian belon – as well as the marron. However, at the top of my list of native seafood I would nominate the barramundi, as well as all our freshwater crayfish – universally known as yabbies, although there are differences.

In his book, *A Salute to the Humble Yabby*, Peter Olszewski distinguishes between river crayfish and yabbies, singling out the Murray cray as the largest of the former group. It's a complicated distinction which you will find carefully explained in his book. But you may be interested to know that there are 388 identified species of freshwater crayfish in Australia.

Down on the farm they'd catch their yabbies in the dam with the old meat and string method (a bit of smelly meat on the end of a piece of string and wait for the yabby to bite) or various elaborate nets. Luckily, today there are professional yabby farms that raise them for you. If your local fish shop doesn't have them, go online.

The word 'yabby' comes from a variety of Indigenous languages, 'yaapitch' in Barababaraba around Kerang; 'yapi' in Wadi Wadi around Swan Hill; and 'yapitch' in Wemba Wemba around Lake Boga.

What is generally meant by the word yabby are the varieties *Cherax destructor* and *Cherax albidus*. They grow up to 150 grams in weight and about 16 centimetres in length (not counting the claws). These critters, mostly the *C. destructor*, can be found in dams and billabongs within a sort of football-shaped area extending from Port Pirie in South Australia up to Mount Isa, then curving across to Charters Towers and down west of the Great Divide to Cape Howe.

Also worth mentioning is the Western Australian marron, *Cherax tenuimanus*, weighing in at a healthy 1.8 kilograms and around 40 centimetres long, with the tail – the edible bit – constituting over 40 per cent of body weight. Peter Olszweski says of the marron it is '… internationally renowned as the sweetest and finest crayfish meat available'.

Then there are the two bugs, the Balmain (*Ibacus peronii*) found mainly in the southern part of the continent and the Moreton Bay (*Thenus orientalis*) across the northern half, also known as Australian bay lobsters. Balmain bugs are usually larger and heavier, both swim backwards when they're in a hurry and bury themselves in sand or mud during the day. In both bugs most of the meat is in the tail. Which has the best flavour? We'll leave that to you.

The magnificent barramundi is an ancient survivor of the Eocene epoch (56 to 34 million years ago). In the wild in Arnhem Land they swim downstream to breed early in the year and then in October and November the young fish swim back upstream to mature. The locals find the best time to spear them is in March and April, during the heavy rains. When the floodwaters recede they get caught in the freshwater billabongs and lay down fat. By mid-June, the fish are found in plentiful numbers north of the Mary River in Queensland and right across to the north of the Ashburton River in central Western Australia.

Of course most of the barramundi you'll see in fish markets and fishmongers these days are farmed, and perhaps the largest and one of the best-known producers is Humpty Doo (see Sources and resources).

Interestingly, barramundi are protandrous hermaphrodites, meaning that the males change sex and become female around the age of five. Very large barras are usually female and are the world's greatest egg carriers – they can produce 17 million eggs in one spawning.

NUTRITIONAL PROPERTIES

All seafood is generally considered to be low in total fat and saturated fat. Most fish and shellfish contain less than 5 per cent total fat, and even the fattiest fish, such as mackerel and king salmon, have no more than 15 per cent fat. A large proportion of the fat in seafood is polyunsaturated, including omega-3 fatty acids, which have added health benefits. Fish is a natural source of B-complex vitamins, vitamin D and vitamin A (especially oily fish). B-complex vitamins have been associated with healthy development of the nervous system. Vitamin A is needed for healthy vision as well as for healthy skin, while vitamin D is essential in bone development. Fish is also a good source of minerals such as selenium, zinc, iodine and iron.

COOKING WITH YABBIES, BUGS AND BARRAMUNDI

You'll love the yabby for its succulent flesh and the ease with which you can cook it. Just boil yabbies for a few minutes, then serve with bread and butter. You can squeeze a little lemon juice over them or vinegar if you prefer. Beer is a traditional accompaniment, wine for the more chi-chi (that's me – I reckon a Clare Valley Riesling). There are recipes that do more to them but in my opinion it's

best not to do too much or their delicate flavour will be drowned.

Bugs can be boiled, baked, or barbecued. To eat, slice the tail (where the meat is) in half long ways, and extract the meat. Anything you can do with a lobster, you can do with a bug. You'll find many recipes for them online, and a cracker here from Mindy Woods.

The raw flesh of the barramundi is pearly pink and turns white when cooked. The flesh is firm, with a moist texture and large flakes, and is prized for its sweet, buttery flavour. The bones are particularly tough in larger fish, and it would be best to get expert help to bone and fillet them (most good fishmongers, especially at a fish market, will do this for you). Wild-caught barra has the best flavour. Baby barra are farmed and have a much milder flavour. That said, they are good when cooked Asian-style – roasted with ginger and soy or steamed with ginger and spring onions.

MINDY WOODS

RED CURRY BAY LOBSTER (BUG) WITH GERALDTON WAX

Serves 3-4

The key to extracting flavour and maintaining protein structure when cooking with crustaceans is just like that of land protein (beef/ lamb/chicken etc): cook it 'on bone' or 'in shell'. Far more flavour, much better structure, and lots of fun getting your hands and fingers involved in the eating process. MW

9–12 fresh green or frozen and thawed bay lobster (Moreton bay or Balmain bugs)
2 tablespoons coconut oil
800 ml coconut milk
800 ml coconut cream, plus extra to serve (optional)
2–4 tablespoons fish sauce
1 tablespoon coconut sugar
2 limes, cut into wedges, plus extra to serve
6 fresh Geraldton Wax sprigs (or makrut lime leaves), picked

Curry paste
30 dried long red chillies, soaked in warm water for at least 30 minutes, then drain, pat dry and coarsely chop
6 small red shallots, peeled and coarsely chopped
60 g native ginger (or galangal or young ginger) coarsely chopped
2 tablespoons coarsely chopped native lemongrass
1 teaspoon ground turmeric
2 garlic cloves, chopped
3 teaspoons shrimp paste, dry roasted in foil
½ bunch coriander stem and roots, scraped and roughly chopped, leaves reserved
30–60 ml vegetable oil

1. For the curry paste, place all the ingredients in a food processor and process to achieve a smooth paste.
2. Gently bend back the middle 'fin' of the bug tail to 'snap it back'. Once loose gently pull on the fin and the entrail should pull away from the flesh. Using a large sharp knife cut it in half. Place in a clean bowl and set aside or refrigerate until ready to use.
3. Heat the coconut oil in a large heavy-based saucepan over medium–high heat.
4. Add the curry paste and stir for 1–2 minutes, until fragrant.
5. Add the coconut milk and coconut cream and bring to a simmer.
6. Add the prepared bugs and cook, stirring occasionally, for 2–4 minutes until the flesh turns opaque.
7. Season with a good splash of fish sauce, a touch of coconut sugar, and freshly squeezed lime.
8. Remove from the heat, transfer to a serving bowl, finish with Geraldton wax, the reserved coriander leaf and a drizzle of coconut cream if desired.
9. Serve with fresh lime wedges and ice-cold lager.

REBECCA SULLIVAN

BARRAMUNDI FILLETS WITH MUNTRIE SALSA

Serves 2

A superbly simple recipe that adds to, but does not detract from, the flavour of fried barra. Based on experience, frying is the best way to cook this magnificent fish.

2 x 200 g barramundi fillets,
   skin on
salt
1 tablespoon olive oil, for shallow-
   frying
2 sea blite sprigs, to garnish

Salsa
150 g muntries (native apples,
   see opposite)
1 small red capsicum, finely diced
2 spring onions, finely chopped
juice of 1 small lemon
dash of apple cider vinegar
1 teaspoon honey (local if possible)
80 ml olive oil
salt and pepper, to taste

1. Remove the fish from the fridge about half an hour before cooking to bring it to room temperature. Pat the barramundi fillets dry using paper towel (I do this with all fish fillets).
2. With a very sharp knife, score the skin, but not the flesh. Do this by making small long cuts along the fillets. Season each side with salt.
3. Heat the olive oil in a non-stick frying pan over medium heat. Place the fillets, skin side down, in the pan, turn up the heat to medium–high and cook for 3–4 minutes until the skin is golden brown.

4. Now turn the fillets and cook for another 2 minutes, or until just cooked through or to your liking. Remove the fish from the pan and let it rest while you make the salsa.
5. To make the salsa, combine all the ingredients in a small bowl and mix thoroughly.
6. Serve the salsa on top of the barramundi with some sea blite to garnish.

. . . .

MUNTRIES

Otherwise known as the native apple or crab apple, the muntrie (*Kunzea pomifera*) grows on a low shrub on the south coast of Australia where the name – a Europeanisation of muntari, adapted from the Kaurna and Ngarrinderi languages of eastern South Australia – comes from. A small purple-green berry that resembles a fig, it is sweet, apple-flavoured with an aroma of moist fruit mince, spice, honey and butter. It is one of the fruits most widely used by non-Indigenous Australians, for pies, chutneys, in fruit salad or to make sweet or savoury sauces.

. . . .

MACROPODS AND MAGPIE GOOSE

KANGAROO AND WALLABY

The kangaroo and the wallaby, magnificent marsupial macropods (macropod meaning 'large foot'), are emblems of and indigenous to Australia. The four main species of kangaroo are the red, the eastern grey, the western grey and the antilopine – the far-northern equivalent of the eastern and western grey kangaroos whose name comes from its antelope-like fur.

Except when describing the Tasmanian Bennetts wallaby, which lives on the mainland in the south-east where it is known as the red-necked wallaby, the word wallaby usually means small kangaroo.

Kangaroos and wallabies are harvested from their native habitat. They are not treated with chemicals, nor do they need to be fed – they simply thrive on the pasture they find. And because of those big soft feet, they're kinder on the land they bound over than farmed animals.

Reputable producers respect quotas, take only males and make sure the animals are killed in export-quality abattoirs.

As a general rule, Indigenous Australians traditionally cooked kangaroo and wallaby in a pit over a fire that had burned down. Pieces were cut off and eaten on the spot.

NUTRITIONAL PROPERTIES

Both kangaroo and wallaby are lean, protein-rich meats high in iron and polyunsaturated fatty acids and low in cholesterol.

COOKING WITH KANGAROO AND WALLABY

Kangaroo and wallaby meat is rich in flavour and slightly gamey (more so if aged) and, when properly cooked, is tender and juicy. Generally, wallaby meat is a richer colour and milder in flavour than kangaroo. Seventeen cuts are taken from the kangaroo and nine from the wallaby. Different cuts require different cooking methods.

Some flavours that go particularly well with kangaroo meat are garlic, rosemary, juniper, Tasmanian pepperberry and regular black pepper, as well as fruity flavours such as plum, red currant, quandong, orange, beetroot and of course red wine.

The striploin is the most popular cut. Because it is so low in fat it needs to be steeped in a good-quality oil before cooking, and then seared in a very hot, heavy-based frying pan or chargrill pan – and when I say very hot, I mean hot as Hades.

The legs of both the kangaroo and the wallaby are the most strongly flavoured and are usually roasted because of their size. Have them boned and rolled, then marinate in oil, red wine, garlic and black pepper and roast at 200°C – 20 minutes per 500 grams. Rest for at least 10 minutes.

Rump can be marinated, seared and then cooked in a

200°C oven – 8 minutes per 500 grams for medium, 4 minutes for rare.

Both kangaroo and wallaby tails can be stewed slowly and turned into soup. Minced kangaroo makes delicious bolognese as well as burgers.

Diced meat (available from a good butcher) can be casseroled or slow-cooked.

The more you cook with macropods the more at ease you will become with their unique qualities and special needs.

· ·

KANGAROOS: CONSERVE OR CULL?

In the previous edition of this book, I asked whether kangaroos were endangered, and concluded that evidence showed they were not. Just three years later, things have become a little more complicated.

On the one hand, you have Adelaide University's Professor David Paton among scientists who have said that their populations had exploded to 45 million since European colonisation, following human actions such as clearing land for pasture and erecting dog-proof fence which controlled the marsupials' predators.

On the other, *ABC News* reported in 2021 that the impact of the drought has caused NSW's population to plummet by more than a quarter, from 17 million in 2016 to 10.5 million in 2020. Other states report similar population losses.

A 2021 article in *The Guardian* raised another issue: the roo as a danger to the environment. It highlights that changing the environment of the semi-arid interior for livestock and the historic culling of dingoes – a natural predator – has given kangaroos an unnatural advantage. As we did in the last edition we have included a balanced article on kangaroo conservation in the Bibliography.

· ·

MAGPIE GOOSE

In *The Oldest Foods on Earth*, I told the story of Richard Gunner, a South Australian farmer, butcher and provedore who deals in, among other things, game meats. He read a story in late 2014 about the impact magpie geese were having on the mango farms of the Northern Territory. These native Australian geese had fallen in love with the new crop and were swooping on the farms when the fruit was ripening. Many farmers were shooting or poisoning them and leaving them to rot.

Gunner sensed an opportunity. He knew how good magpie geese tasted, and he knew he could find a market for them in the south. And he also had contacts with the Larrakia people on whose lands around Darwin there were both geese and mango farms.

Today, Richard is a minority stakeholder in Something Wild, a company whose general manager is ex-AFL footballer and Larrakia man Daniel Motlop. Gunner says that Motlop and his family will be able to help tell the stories about bush foods as well as work respectfully with Aboriginal communities.

Something Wild sells meats such as kangaroo, wallaby, crocodile, venison, wild boar and buffalo as well as native greens, fruits and outback seasonings. Gunner said:

> We still want to be involved in this but we've taken a step back to have a minority stake. It's the right way to develop the business and it's going to be a lot easier in terms of working with other communities. Daniel works as an adviser for Aboriginal affairs in the Territory, so he knows the people he'll be working with.

And we lucky people in the south can now get the luscious magpie goose as well as all those other bush foods from the north. You can find Something Wild's address (they do mail order) in Sources and resources.

NUTRITIONAL PROPERTIES

No specific data available.

AVAILABLE FORMS

Sadly, at the time of writing, you are likely to get only frozen breast meat which will cook more quickly but with less flavour and texture than fresh.

COOKING WITH MAGPIE GOOSE

The magpie goose is a waterfowl and the only member of its species within one genus. Its name, *Anseranas semipalmata*, is combined Latin for goose, anser, and duck, anas.

For the table, the magpie goose is best cut into legs, thigh and breast and seared in a hot skillet with just a little oil and seasoning, then rested. Breast meat needs only a short searing, the muscle meat of the thighs and legs needs longer.

JEAN-PAUL BRUNETEAU

....

ROAST RUMP OF KANGAROO

Serves 3

The technique in this recipe will stand you in good stead for cooking a rump. If the one you buy is too thick, slice it in half lengthways. It's a delicious combination with the deep heat of the pepperberry sauce.

1 x 400–500 g kangaroo rump
250 ml extra virgin olive oil
freshly ground black pepper (pepper is the best seasoning
    for kangaroo and wallaby meat)
Pepperberry sauce (see page 32), to serve

1. Preheat the oven to 225°C.
2. Marinate the kangaroo in the olive oil for about 1 hour (overnight is fine – but expect a little of the olive flavour to come through, with a slight discolouration of the meat).
3. Heat a heavy-based (black steel or cast iron) ovenproof frying pan over high heat. It needs to be very hot before you add the meat.
4. Take the rump out of the oil and place it directly into the pan. Sprinkle the rump with a generous amount of black pepper, then turn the meat to seal it all over.
5. Reduce the oven temperature to 200°C and place the frying pan in the oven. Cook for 8 minutes for medium, or for 4 minutes for a rarer rump.
6. Let the meat stand in a warm place, for the same length of time as it was cooked.
7. Serve the kangaroo with the pepperberry sauce.

RAYMOND KERSH

OKAH-COATED KANGAROO FILLET

Serves 3

*This twice-cooked method produces a very tender kangaroo.
The okah is Ray's Australian take on dukkah. You can also eat the
okah alone, with crusty bread and olive or macadamia oil.*

600 g kangaroo fillets
salt and pepper, to taste
2 egg whites
75 g plain flour
olive oil, for shallow-frying

Macadamia and candlenut okah
50 g macadamia nuts, chopped
25 g shredded coconut

25 g cumin seeds
25 g fresh breadcrumbs made
   from day-old bread
25 g coriander seeds
15 g fennel seeds
50 g candlenuts
¼ teaspoon hot paprika
sea salt, to taste

1. To make the okah, preheat the oven to 180°C.
2. Combine all the ingredients, except the paprika and salt, on a baking tray lined with baking paper, then toast the mixture in the oven for 5–8 minutes, until fragrant. Set aside and allow to cool.
3. In a food processor, blitz the mixture until coarsely ground. Add the paprika and sea salt.
4. Take the kangaroo fillets out of any packaging and dry them. Season lightly and set aside.

5. Whisk the egg whites and flour into a paste.
6. Paint the paste along the top side of the kangaroo fillets, then coat that side with the okah.
7. Put some olive oil in a heavy-based (see Roast rump of kangaroo, page 111) frying pan over high heat. When very hot, place the kangaroo fillets in the pan, okah side down. Cook for around 2 minutes until the okah is crisp and brown.
8. Turn the kangaroo over in the pan, then transfer the pan to the pre-heated oven and cook for 4 minutes – if the fillet is extra thick, cook it for a further 2 minutes.
9. Remove the kangaroo from the oven and let it rest for a few minutes, then slice it and serve hot.

Note: It is essential to only cook kangaroo until it is rare or medium–rare. This is best achieved by using a really hot pan or oven or, like this recipe, twice-cooking.

Tip: Unless your pan has a detachable handle, be very careful when taking it out of the oven not to burn yourself.

REBECCA SULLIVAN

KANGAROO SIZZLERS WITH FINGER LIME

Serves 4–6

*The first bush foods dish I ate was Phillip Searle's kangaroo
with pickled beetroot, which introduced me to the principle of
partnering 'roo with tart flavours. Rebecca follows this principle by
using both finger and desert limes.*

1 kg kangaroo striploin or fillet
olive oil, for drizzling
salt and freshly ground black pepper, to taste
Warndu Native Thyme Oil (see Note)
Warndu Wattleseed Balsamic (see Note)
juice of ½ lemon
4–6 finger limes, caviar squeezed out
100 g desert limes, to garnish, chopped
100 g muntries (native apples, see page 105), whole
native thyme leaves or micro herbs, to garnish

1. Take the kangaroo out of the fridge an hour before cooking to bring
    it to room temperature. Place it on a plate and drizzle both sides with
    olive oil.
2. Heat a frying pan over high heat until almost smoking. Place the
    kangaroo in the pan and seal it all on sides until golden brown.
    Remove it from the pan and leave to rest until cool to the touch.
3. Using a very sharp knife, slice the meat as thinly as possible.

4. Arrange the meat on a serving platter and season. Drizzle over the native thyme oil, balsamic and lemon juice. Sprinkle the finger lime caviar over the slices and add the desert limes, muntries and herbs as garnish.

Note: Warndu is an online store specialising in bush-food ingredients. See Sources and resources to find out where you can buy their thyme oil and balsamic, together with finger limes, desert limes and muntries.

• •

AUSTRALIAN NATIVE THYME (*PROSTANTHERA INCISA*)

This plant, also known as round-leaf mint, cut-leaf mint or native oregano, has an earthy, strongly aromatic minty flavour and is native to south-east New South Wales, eastern Victoria and Tasmania. The herb has long been used by Indigenous people for its medicinal properties. The bush grows to 2 metres, with a showy display of lilac flowers on the tips in spring. Use native thyme with kangaroo, chicken, turkey, pork or lamb.

• •

JEAN-PAUL BRUNETEAU

SEARED MAGPIE GOOSE BREASTS

Serves – 1 breast per person

I first ate magpie goose at Jean-Paul's restaurant, Riberries, in the mid-1990s. He had managed to get hold of some birds when it was difficult to do so, and simply seared the breast legs and thighs. I said at the time that this was the best poultry I had ever tasted, even better than my favourite, duck. I've waited a long time for more magpie goose to become available. At the time of writing you're more likely to get breasts than whole birds.

1 magpie goose or one set of goose breasts
salt and white pepper
150 ml olive oil
½ teaspoon sesame oil

1. If you're working with a whole bird remove the legs (you can confit them or roast them separately) and ease the breast meat off the rib cage using a sharp fillet knife. If you've bought the breast meat from Something Wild, proceed from here.
2. Rub salt and pepper onto the breast skin and flesh.
3. Heat a heavy-based frying pan, pour in the oils and sear the breast 7 minutes on the skin side, 4 minutes on the other side.
4. Let the breast stand for 8–10 minutes before slicing.
5. Serve with the condiments you'd use for duck or turkey.

MOTLOP FAMILY RECIPE

....

BARBECUED MAGPIE GOOSE SKEWERS

Makes 6 skewers

*Daniel Motlop sent us this recipe, an example
of Indigenous–Asian fusion from the Top End.*

500 g magpie goose breast

Marinade

50 g crushed peanuts (or 100 g
    crushed macadamias and skip
    peanut butter)

50 g smooth peanut butter

½ teaspoon curry powder

50 ml light soy sauce

2 garlic cloves, crushed

10 g crushed fresh root ginger

juice of ½ lime

50 ml kecap manis

25 g fried shallots

25 ml peanut (or macadamia) oil

1. Assemble marinade ingredients and mix thoroughly.
2. Cut the breast into 3 cm cubes.
3. Add the breast to the marinade and leave in the fridge for 4 hours or overnight.
4. Slide the breast pieces onto wooden or steel skewers.
5. Heat the remaining marinade.
6. Barbecue or grill the skewers until just cooked.
7. Serve with the heated leftover marinade poured over the skewers.

*Daniel Motlop is a Larrakia man and former Australian Rules footballer. More
recently Daniel has embarked on a career as a food and beverage entrepreneur
and is the general manager and part-owner, with his family, of bush food
business Something Wild. See Sources and resources.*

ANDREW FIELKE

BRAISED WALLABY SHANKS WITH OLIVES AND BUSH TOMATO

Serves 4

*Andrew takes his wallaby to the Mediterranean and then brings it
back home with the bush tomato. A simple and sensational dish.
Serve with mashed potato, polenta or even risotto.*

8 small wallaby shanks

75 g plain flour, for dusting

2 dessertspoons extra virgin olive
oil

15 g butter

1 large carrot, peeled and cut into
2 cm pieces

1 large celery stalk, cut into 2 cm
pieces

100 g kalamata olives, pitted

4 garlic cloves, peeled

1 large onion, peeled

250 ml red wine

1 litre beef stock

500 ml tomato passata or purée

1 teaspoon dried wild thyme
(or a few sprigs of fresh)

1 teaspoon ground pepperberry
leaf (or black pepper)

1 teaspoon sea salt

2 bay leaves

35 g whole dried bush tomatoes,
coarsely chopped (3–5 mm
pieces)

2 tablespoons chopped fresh
sea parsley, to garnish

1. Dust the wallaby shanks with flour, shaking off the excess.
2. Heat the olive oil and butter in a saucepan over medium heat, add the shanks to the pan and brown them all over.
3. Add the carrot and celery to the pan, and cook for a few minutes, until caramelised. Add the remaining ingredients, except the sea parsley, to the pan. Cover and bring to the boil.
4. Reduce the heat and leave to simmer very gently for 1½–2 hours, until the shanks are quite tender and the meat is almost falling off the bone.
5. If the sauce needs reducing, remove the shanks from the pan and cook the sauce until thickened.
6. Garnish the shanks and their sauce with the sea parsley, then serve.

GRAINS AND RICE: THE FUTURE

Although we have come a very long way in the time since I first wrote *The Oldest Foods on Earth*, this does not apply in some categories, especially native grains and rices.

Space dictated the number of foods I could cover in this small book and they were selected on the basis of their popularity, use and (relative) ease of purchase. Although you can now find finger limes in season and lemon myrtle in many if not most greengrocers and supermarkets, the rest require persistence.

And patience. As I keep reminding myself, we non-Indigenous Australians have ignored the food of this land – and its first people – for a good 200 of the 230 years we have been here. We've got some catching up to do. Especially in two areas. Firstly, wild grasses, some of the most important foods for Indigenous people.

Wild grasses/grains. The wheat we eat today started out as grass. Over thousands of years it was selectively bred to improve and grow the ears of the grasses so that they could be more easily harvested and processed.

For thousands of years, Indigenous Australians across vast areas of the country propagated seeds, irrigated crops and harvested and stored the native grasses that still grow wild.

Bruce Pascoe, author of *Dark Emu*, tells the story of the grindstones used for grinding seeds to flour, which were found at Cuddie Springs in northern New South Wales. They were dated as being around 30 000 years old. Pascoe points out that this was some 15 000 years before the Egyptians started baking bread from flour, making Indigenous Australians the first to bake bread.

When I first wrote this book, I contacted Dr Angela Pattison, a plant breeder and agricultural scientist with the University of Sydney Institute of Agriculture at Narrabri who was about to begin a major project researching Indigenous agriculture. It is now well under way.

'When I read *The Oldest Foods on Earth*, *Dark Emu* and *The Biggest Estate on Earth* [by Bill Gammage]' Dr Pattison told me:

> I thought, if this is how it used to be [Indigenous agricultural practice] we need to re-create it, figure out how it works and see what elements of what used to be can be used in a modern context … and what can we

do to bring back the methods that have worked well and sustainably for thousands of years in Australia.

At the start of NAIDOC Week in November 2020, Dr Pattison and her colleagues launched the first report from a feasibility study into using native grass grains as a modern food product. And initial findings look promising. (See Bibliography for details.)

Conducted on Gamilaraay and Yuwaalaraay Country in north-west NSW, the one-year research project examined the environmental, economic and cultural viability of growing native grains for bread.

'[This region] is one of the largest Aboriginal language groups in Australia, and they are proudly known as grass people,' Dr Pattison explained. Today, home to some of Australia's best-quality agricultural land producing non-native crops (such as cotton and wheat), historically the region produced native grains (dhunbarr), such as Mitchell grass and native millet, which were ground up and made into fire-roasted bread (dhuwarr) by traditional owners for thousands of years.

The team has collaborated with Black Duck, founded by Bruce Pascoe and has brought together experts in ecology, food science, social science, marketing and business to work on different parts of the paddock-to-plate system as it might work on Gamilaraay Country.

'Forging a path forward for our food production systems, which is environmentally, economically and culturally sustainable, is one of the biggest challenges of our time,' Dr Pattison said.

This one-year paddock-to-plate trial, done in collaboration with both local Aboriginal community members and farmers, seeking to find a way forward for the good of people and the good of the planet is not long enough to solve problems hundreds of years in the making. But the report, and set of webinars, will hopefully bring holders of knowledge together to make a start.

Aunty Bernadette, local Aboriginal Elder coordinator of the Garragal Women's Language and Culture Network at Toomelah, said: 'If we start producing our own grains and flour it's going to help, especially our old people who've been living for decades on all the white flour, salt and fat. When they go back and eat traditional food and drink traditional herbal teas they get better.'

Rices. Two of the four Australian native rices are considered the best varieties for research and development. *Oryza rufipogon* and *O. meridionalis* were an abundant and widespread resource in floodplains across monsoonal Australia and were harvested and consumed by the Indigenous population for thousands of years.

Today, researchers are reporting that these wild rices growing in northern Australia's wetlands could help boost global food security – and become an important food crop.

Valuable traits from the wild rice – such as drought tolerance and pest and disease resistance – can be bred into commercial rice strains to boost global rice production. Australian wild rice could be cultivated as a tasty and nutritious product in its own right.

What has stopped progress in the past is that commercial interests have to be convinced there's a value return for them. It costs millions of dollars to breed a new cultivar and they've got to be sure they're going to get a single variety out of it.

But recently the Australian Government agreed to fund the Future Food Systems Cooperative Research Centre (CRC), which is expected to include a $1.8 million project for Darwin's Charles Darwin University (CDU) to develop commercially viable native rice as an agri-business.

CDU Research Institute for the Environment and Livelihoods (RIEL) researchers Dr Sean Bellairs and Dr Penny Wurm said the expected value of the CDU native rice project would be more than $200 000 in funding a year for the next decade.

CDU has been working on a native rice project for many years, but with this funding, they believe they can put Darwin on the map as a major producer of a range of native rices.

Dr Wurm said the project aimed to produce the rice on land near Fogg Dam owned by Pudakul Aboriginal Cultural Tours, a long-term partner with CDU researchers.

KERRIE SAUNDERS

....

NATIVE GRAIN PIZZA

A deliberately simple (and forgiving!) recipe to make practising with native grain flours easy and fun, whether you are an accomplished chef making a gourmet meal or cooking a regular dinner with kids. Feel free to adapt to your liking, including making a version which rises with yeast, uses proper bread/pizza flour instead of plain flour, adds a bit of milk or sugar, or uses gluten free ingredients (the suggested native grain flours below are gluten free). Start with a 1:3 ratio of native to conventional flour, then experiment to taste. Gamilaraay/Yuwaalayaay words are used for the ingredients below. KS

(This is, I believe, the first native grain recipe published. JN)

Base

- ⅓ cup ganalay (Mitchell grass) flour (see note)
- 1 cup plain flour (plus extra, for dusting)
- 2 teaspoon baking powder
- 1 teaspoon salt
- 2 teaspoon olive oil
- ½ cup water

Toppings

- 50 g salt-free tomato paste
- 1 tablespoon ground *gumi* (bush tomato) (see note)
- ¾ cup grated cheese
- Seasonal native greens, such as *dhamu* (purslane), *galaan galaan* (warrigal greens) and *binamaya* (old man saltbush) (see note)
- Seasonal native fruits, such as *burra* (ruby saltbush) or *gayn gayn* (desert lime)

1. Preheat the oven to fan-forced 200°C.
2. Sift the dry base ingredients together.
3. Add the olive oil, then add most of the water.
4. Mix into a dough ball, then add more water until the dough is just sticky. The amount of water required will depend on what flour you use. If you add too much water, just add 1 tablespoon extra flour.
5. Tip the ball onto a floured benchtop and knead the ball until the dough is smooth. Pizza bases do not require kneading to the same extent as bread dough – the ingredients just need to be smooth.
6. Roll the dough to the shape of your non-stick pizza pan or stone and position ready to cook. Squeeze the edges up to make a puffy crust if desired.
7. Mix the bush tomato and tomato paste in a bowl, then spread over the base.
8. Top with seasonal native toppings, then cheese. (You may like to brush the exposed crust edges with oil to help them crisp up.)
9. Place in the oven, checking after 10 minutes. The pizza is ready when the crust is crispy and golden.
11. Cut and serve.

Note: Mitchell grass flour can be substituted with ground binamaya (old man saltbush) seed, which is much easier to source. Salt is not required if binamaya flour is used.

You may like to purchase a bush tomato chutney from your favourite native food supplier for the base instead of a mix of tomato paste and bush tomato. Or experiment by adding low-salt barbecue sauce too.

We like to use local native toppings, and we find that native greens from Gomeroi Country don't shrivel up like baby spinach in the oven.

Kerrie Saunders is a Kamilaroi/Gomeroi woman working with Angela Pattison at the University of Sydney, Narrabri. She also runs cultural and bush food tours at Moree with her company Yinarr-ma, which can be found on Facebook, where people can do a tour to taste native grass grains.

ACKNOWLEDGMENTS

FIRST AND ALWAYS TO THE INDIGENOUS PEOPLE OF THIS LAND FOR THEIR MORE THAN 60 000 YEARS OF STEWARDSHIP AND CARE OF THAT LAND, WHICH HAS SHOWN THE REST OF US THE WAY. ALWAYS WAS, ALWAYS WILL BE ABORIGINAL LAND.

For helping us to understand their foods and bring them into our kitchens, thanks go to the two non-Indigenous bush food pioneers Vic Cherikoff and Jean-Paul Bruneteau. Without the work of these two we would not have had the foundations on which to build a bush foods industry. And a special thanks to Jean-Paul for his book *Tukka* — not just for the recipes generously given to me for use in this book, but for information in the text, which proved invaluable in my research. As I have written before in this book, if you find a copy of *Tukka*, buy it.

For their years of dedication and invention using bush foods in the kitchens of their Edna's Table restaurants, chef Raymond Kersh and his sister and partner in creativity, Jennice. While writing this book, in typically generous style Ray Kersh offered me numerous recipes that he had created for Kenvale College of Tourism and Hospitality Management. These recipes were delivered in classes conducted by Ray and Jennice for high school teachers to take back to their schools and pass on to their students for use in home kitchens.

ACKNOWLEDGMENTS

My thanks also to:

Fiona Porteous who represents the next stage of bush foods producers: her focus is on the home kitchen.

Rebecca Sullivan, a chef, producer and mover and shaker in the industry who has been generous with her time in helping me with this book.

Amanda Garner, the general manager of First Nations Bushfoods and Botanical Alliance Australia (FNBBAA), the body that represents all interests in the industry. But more than that, Amanda has a deep understanding and knowledge of bush food and producers, from the kitchen to country. She has been invaluable in helping me find my way around the bush food industry. And finally to all who gave me permission to use recipes from their commercial or home kitchens, thank you:

Paula Nihot
Mindy Woods
Kerrie Saunders
Jill Dupleix
Paul Van Reyk
Andrew Fielke
Gayle Quarmby
Bret Cameron
Neville Bonney
Jude Mayall
Simon Bryant
Dan Churchill
Peter Olszewski
Rosemary Sinclair
Daniel Motlop
Jean-Paul Bruneteau
Rebecca Sullivan
Fiona Porteous
Raymond Kersh

SOURCES AND RESOURCES

The information here was current at time of writing but may change. That is, some sources may drop by the wayside, and others may spring up. It is a dynamic market.

In addition to these specialist sites and suppliers, more and more Australian bush food produce and products are creeping into supermarkets, greengrocers and butchers. Keep your eyes open for them.

Alpine Game Meats, based in Prospect, Sydney, supplies nutritious, chemical-free whole foods that are wild-harvested and free-range where possible. The company's product range includes kangaroo, wallaby, crocodile, wild boar, emu, game birds, game sausages, buffalo, camel and possum. <www.alpinegamemeats.com>

Australian Fungi is a fascinating site that offers extensive information on the various native Australian fungi, and information on their use by Indigenous people. <www.anbg.gov.au/fungi>

Australian Native Food and Botanicals (ANFAB) is the peak national body that represents all interests in the rapidly growing Australian bush food and botanical industry. (ANFAB previously operated as ANFIL – Australian Native Food Industry Limited). Here you will find the most comprehensive list of suppliers and producers in the country, many of whom you will be able to approach with your produce questions. <www.anfab.org.au>

Australian Native Food Co This South Australian based business is focussed on the use of local fresh products and produce as well as supporting local communities. They use the highest quality and freshest ingredients in a range of ready to eat food products sourced from local suppliers only. Although the business is not Indigenous owned, 70 per cent of their employees are Indigenous and they support community, local farmers and growers. <www.australiannativefoodco.com.au>

The Australian Superfood Co retails a wide range of processed and ready-to-use Australian bush food products in accordance with their principles: 'We hope to encourage self-reliance and prosperity in Indigenous communities by sourcing our products from them and by directing a percentage of our profits to the improvement of education and health in the communities'. <www.austsuperfoods.com.au>

Bent Shed Produce is the company run by Fiona Porteous and Peter Micallef. They grow, source and create a range of produce and products in their Tarago property (thirty minutes south of Goulburn, New South Wales), specialising in Australian bush foods and bush-ranged poultry products. They also provide information and training on the growing and use of Australian bush foods in everyday cooking. Products can be ordered by email or look for their stall at local markets. If you're lucky enough to be near one, go and talk to Fiona as she offers a wealth of information. <info@bentshedproduce.com.au> <www.bentshedproduce.com.au>

Brookfarm is a macadamia product supplier, run by the Brook family. Their macadamia oil is far and away the best in the author's opinion. <www.brookfarm.com.au>

Brookie's Byron Slow Gin is made from Davidson plums picked from trees planted outside the distillery, which is situated in the Brook family's 40-hectare farm in the hinterland of Byron Bay. The distillery itself rests among the macadamia orchard and rainforest that the Brooks have regenerated. <www.capebyrondistillery.com>

Vic Cherikoff is rightly credited as a non-Indigenous pioneer of the Australian wild food industry. As a scientist, author and entrepreneur he has put his degree in applied biology to work in developing bioactive resources, including unique flavour blends, freeze-dried wild food ingredients, antimicrobials, super-nutritionals and more. These ingredients have grown from bush tucker to bush food, native foods and now wild foods. <www.cherikoff.net>

Chocolate on Purpose Wiradjuri woman Fiona Harrison and her 'mudyibang' (friend and supporter) Jo create a chocolate range called Bush Food Chocolate. It's a fusion of the finest Belgian chocolate and the best of Australian native botanicals such as Garal (Wattleseed), Boombera (Macadamia Nut), Gulalung (Finger Limes), Wyrrung (Wild Rosella) and many others. <www.chocolateonpurpose.com.au>

Andrew Fielke, bush foods expert, has expanded his footprint. He now offers products and produce to both the hospitality industry and the home cook from his new base, a warehouse in Hindmarsh, South Australia – Creative Native Food Service and Tuckeroo Retail Products. Andrew and his team have brought together producers and consumers to promote native produce and raise awareness of seasonality, availability, cultural heritage and unique characteristics. <creativenativefoods.com.au/shop/>

First Nations Bushfoods & Botanical Alliance Australia is a newly formed national body committed to ensure the development of a thriving and fully Indigenous owned bush foods and botanicals industry. A Board has been appointed consisting of key Indigenous people representing the States and Territories who are authorised to make representation at political levels as well as with relevant authorities, bodies and stakeholders in relation to First Nation involvement in the industry. This will lead to innovative Indigenous-led solutions across the industry and is a good resource to find the best Indigenous bush food businesses. <fnbbaa.com.au>

Humpty Doo is the largest saltwater barramundi farm in the country, on the banks of the Northern Territory's Adelaide River halfway between Darwin and Kakadu. They provide good information as well as recipes and can tell you where your nearest supplier is. <www.humptydoobarramundi.com.au>

Indigiearth is an Aboriginal-owned and operated business, which is well established in Mudgee in central-west New South Wales. It was started by Sharon Winsor, a Ngemba Weilwan woman of western New South Wales. Sharon, born in Gunnedah, turned her childhood pastime of collecting and eating bush fruits – at first a necessity – into a thriving business selling Indigiearth-branded jams, spice mixes and other native plant products. <www.indigiearth.com.au>

Kurrajong Australian Native Foods use a variety of Australian native herbs, spices, fruits and nuts to make their unique jams, conserves, sauces and spices. These ingredients are sourced from sustainable growers in many regions of Australia. <www.bushtuckershop.com>

Lenah Game Meats produces high-quality Tasmanian game meats and has been specialising in wallaby for over twenty years. It is a small, privately owned Tasmanian company founded by John and Katrina Kelly and Sally Bruen in 1993. Lenah are committed to making the world a better place socially, environmentally and ecologically. The site offers recipes, cuts and interstate suppliers. <www.lenah.com.au>

Mayi Harvests Native Foods was established in 2006 as an Indigenous cooperative, to supply wild-harvested Kakadu Plum 'Gabiny' and other native fruits and seeds. Traditional methods of wild harvesting throughout the six seasons found in the Kimberley of Western Australia are followed. All produce is hand-picked according to the season. Frozen produce is freshly frozen, and dried produce is either sun-dried, roasted and ground. Mayi supplies a wide range of premium quality bush foods that can be purchased in small batches or bulk wholesale orders. All produce can be used for food, drinks or cosmetic purposes. <mayiharvests. com.au>

Melbourne Bushfood offers a wide range of herbs and spices, jams, bush food vitamins and plants. Not First-Nations owned but, like many of today's bush foods businesses, they work extensively with a range of Indigenous communities to bring their products to market while ensuring appropriate benefit sharing schemes are in place. Currently 50 per cent of their suppliers are Aboriginal owned, and they are expanding that (see also Grow your own). <melbournebushfood.com.au>

Natif works directly with Indigenous communities to help them establish bush food volume and establishing accounts in which they can grow into the future. They visit growers and harvesters around Australia. Native fruits are freeze dried in a HACCP facility in Victoria, which supports local jobs in their community. Their website states that they 'value the importance of evidence based and traditional information about bush foods, where they come from, how they are processed, the method and ethics of collection and rights of the Indigenous people who collect some of this food, including their IP'. <natif.com.au>

OutbackChef has been an Australian native herb and spice company since 2005. Now it's one of Australia's leading suppliers of native herbs, spices, fruits and berries to the hospitality industry and home cooks. They work directly with wild-harvesters, Indigenous communities, farmers and growers in regional and remote areas. <www.outbackchef.com.au>

Outback Spirit are producers of a range of Australian bush food products, also working in partnership with Aboriginal communities. <www.outbackspirit.com.au>

Paroo Kangaroo originated in the Paroo Darling region in far west New South Wales, an area known for its mostly untouched land and abundance of native vegetation. Paroo kangaroo is sourced from only the finest wild game kangaroos from specific regions. The website offers very good information on kangaroo cuts as well as simple recipes. <www.parookangaroo.com.au>

Quarmby Horticulture is the business run by Mike and Gayle Quarmby. In 1996, Mike and Gayle set up the Reedy Creek Nursery in South Australia, the source of the bush food produce sold under the Outback Pride brand.

With the facilities at Reedy Creek Nursery, the Quarmbys were able to undertake extensive research and development on the commercial viability and production of up to sixty-five native foods species. They covered 950 000 kilometres, visiting, mentoring and setting up small gardens in remote communities. 'The Elders showed us the best plants and we took plant material and propagated plants to take back to those communities,' Gayle explains. In addition to the most viable species of native foods they planted in the nursery, they also planted 500 000 plants at Indigenous community sites.

As part of the long-term vision of the Outback Pride Project, the ownership of Reedy Creek Nursery Pty Ltd, Outback Pride Fresh and Outback Pride Grocery has been handed to First Nation ownership. This was always their intention.

With their new business, Quarmby Horticulture, the Quarmbys are continuing valuable research and development into the sustainable production of native food plants, on a consultancy basis. As I write this, they're building a website. In the meantime feel free to email them with any queries.<quarmbyhort@gmail.com>

Sobah is Aboriginal owned and led and is Australia's first non-alcoholic craft beer company based on Yugambeh country known as the Gold Coast, Queensland. Their brews include Lemon Aspen Pilsner, Finger Lime Cerveza and Pepperberry IPA. I have tried the Pepperberry IPA and would never have believed it was alcohol-free unless I was told.
<www.sobah.com.au>

Something Wild is where you'll find wild and game meats from magpie goose to crocodile and everything in between. At the time of writing, re-construction of this business (and the website) is being undertaken. If you live in Adelaide, visit their stand at the Central Market. Or to order from elsewhere call the stall on (07) 8410 7322 during market hours. <www.somethingwild.com.au>

Taste Australia Bush Food Shop is a well-stocked online shop stocking over thirty ingredients, products and plants since 2008. <www.bushfoodshop.com.au>

Warndu is the native food company of multi-talented pair, Rebecca Sullivan and Damien Coulthard. Rebecca is the cook and marketing mastermind, Damien is from Adnyamathanha country and grew up in Quorn and Nepabunna in South Australia. He's a teacher and artist and, in Warndu, his role incorporates direct relationship-building with communities and wild-harvesters. This is important for the company as its core goal is to build long-term relationships with communities around Australia. You'll find they have foods, their famous 'roo broth, teas and recipes and more. <www.warndu.com>

GROW YOUR OWN

Here is a list of selected nurseries from each state that offer Australian native plants. You can find additional sources by searching the first two websites listed below.

Australian Native Plants Society (Australia) caters for people interested in Australia's native flora. Their website is a goldmine of information for anyone interested in finding native plants for food or for the garden. <www.anpsa.org.au>

Tucker Bush stocks a range of edible native plants, bringing a uniquely Australian flavour to the modern suburban garden. They're a wholesaler, but there is a list of nurseries they work with on their website. <www.tuckerbush.com.au>

NEW SOUTH WALES

Australian Natives is an invaluable online resource. For almost 25 years, horticulturist Mark Ferrington has offered quality Australian native plants to the public with expert advice. Now that his retail outlet has closed, he is still supplying plants and designing gardens for clients all over Sydney. <www.australian-natives.com.au>

Daley's in Kyogle is a walk-in nursery as well as an online seller, with a wide range of native food plants. <www.daleysfruit.com.au>

Harvest Seeds specialises in growing provenance and local Sydney plants as well as a wide range of Australian plants with a focus on drought-tolerant species and grasses. This was originally a wholesale nursery, but a new owner is moving into retail and is now stocked up with a large number of native food plants. <www.harvestseeds-nativeplants.com.au>

Muru Mittigar Provenance Nursery is a wholesale and retail nursery at Llandilo in Sydney's outer west, specialising in growing indigenous provenance stock in forestry tubes – trees, shrubs, climbers and grasses. Muru Mittigar Ltd aims to employ and train local Indigenous people. Staff training is integral to the success of the nursery, with all members of staff gaining expertise in seed collection, propagation, bush regeneration and traditional plant usage. They have a good range of native produce plants. <www.murumittigar.com.au/provenance-nursery>

Sydney Wildflower Nursery provides the finest-quality Australian plants. Qualified staff and the huge plant range will help you create your own native garden. The nursery, at Heathcote in Sydney, has a good range of native produce plants. <www.sydneywildflowernursery.com.au>

NORTHERN TERRITORY

Arnhem Nursery is one of the largest stockists of tropical plants in Northern Australia and is set in the heart of 2 hectares of lush tropical gardens. The owners have lived onsite since 1978, developing the nursery within the garden of the property. They stock a good range of native food plants and trees and have very good knowledge of their stock. <www.arnhemnursery. com.au>

Maningrida Wild Foods sells wild-harvested native foods that have been sourced by Aboriginal people in the Maningrida region of Arnhem Land for thousands of years. Maningrida Wild Foods mixes traditional cultural knowledge with social enterprise. They follow the guidance of senior Aboriginal people, holders of deep cultural and environmental knowledge. They create opportunities for land and sea owners to generate income from their Country and natural resources. Their work enables people to live or spend time on their clan estates, keep their cultural connections with bush foods alive, promote the consumption of healthy foods in the community and provides an important stream of financial income. <www. maningridawildfoods.com>

Tropiculture Australia is a large nursery specialising in food plants and trees, with a good selection of native food trees in stock. Although open as a retail outlet only on Saturdays from 8 am to 12 pm, they're more than happy to answer queries at other times.

QUEENSLAND

Barung Landcare's Native Plant Nursery stocks around 200 species of native plants and specialises in local rainforest species. It also has a good range of native food plants. <www. barunglandcare.org.au>

Yuruga Nursery in Walkamin, on the Atherton Tablelands, stocks what they claim is Australia's largest range of tropical native plants, as well as a great variety of exotics and fruit trees. They also have a Bush Tucker section, which specialises in those food plants native to northern Queensland. <www.yuruga. com.au>

SOUTH AUSTRALIA

Coromandel Native Nursery is one of South Australia's biggest native nurseries located in Coromandel East. They specialise in Australian native plants in all their various forms and varieties. The nursery carries a good range of native food plants and they are happy to source them for you if they don't have them in stock. <www. natives.net.au/CNNMain.html>

Provenance Indigenous Plants can supply a wide range of trees, shrubs, groundcovers, climbers, grasses and wetland plants. All are indigenous to the Adelaide area, having thrived in that region for thousands of years. Plants are grown in full sun and raised from locally collected seeds or cuttings, and so are perfectly adapted to the local climate and soils. Although not a large selection, all the food plants they stock are indigenous to the coast, plains and foothills. <www.provenance.net.au>

Waite Arboretum in Adelaide is a good research resource for the native food gardener. <www.adelaide.edu.au/waite-historic/arboretum/collections>

TASMANIA

Habitat Plants specialise in growing Tasmanian native plants. They grow for any situation where original Tasmanian vegetation is needed and stock a good collection of Tasmanian native food plants. <www.habitatplants.com.au>

Plants of Tasmania Nursery at Ridgeway, just south-west of Hobart, specialises in growing and selling plants native to Tasmania. They stock over 500 different species and varieties and now have a range of native plants from mainland Australia too. Owner John Gibson worked with author Rees Campbell on the book *Eat Wild Tasmanian* (see the Bibliography). <www.potn.com.au>

VICTORIA

Austplant Nursery and Gardens is set on top of picturesque Arthurs Seat on the Mornington Peninsula. It features over 3 hectares of display gardens ready to be explored. Austplant has over 600 species of native and indigenous plants, a garden design service and hands-on specialist advice. They have a very good range of food plants, as well as a deep interest in them. <www.austplant.com.au>

Kuranga Native Nursery located at the foothills of the Dandenong Ranges, carries a wide range of Australian native plants, including food plants, which are incorporated into the menu at the Paperbark Café and gift shop. <www.kuranga.com.au/native-nursery>

Native Home, House of Plants at Abbotsford has an extensive range of native food plants and advice. <www.facebook.com/nativehomehouseofplants>

Melbourne Bushfood stocks an impressive range of bush food and other native plants with $9.95 flat rate shipping for Australia and New Zealand. <melbournebushfood.com.au>

Willum Warrain Bush Nursery is a 100 per cent Aboriginal community run and owned nursery specialising in native plants indigenous to the Mornington Peninsula. They seek to share knowledge about plants from a cultural perspective with the broader community. This social enterprise creates employment opportunities for local Aboriginal people based around plant sales, bush foods and botanicals. Go to the website for details. <willumwarrain.org.au>

WESTERN AUSTRALIA

Australian Native Nursery has been helping Western Australians get the most from their gardens for nearly twenty years. At their Oakford nursery they grow over 2500 Australian native plant species – as tubestock and up to 23 litre rocket pots. They claim to have the best selection of native food plants in Western Australia. <www.australiannativenursery.com.au>

Supreme Plants is a nursery in the heart of the Swan Valley where plants are grown onsite in the full elements of the weather, to ensure they are strong, healthy plants for Western Australian conditions. <www.supremeplants.com.au>

Zanthorrea Nursery is situated in the hills outside Perth and specialises in native plants of all kinds, with a good range of native food plants. <www.zanthorrea.com>

BIBLIOGRAPHY

BOOKS

Those books that are out of print can usually be found by searching Australian online bookstores.

Bonney, Neville, *Jewel of the Australian Desert: Native peach (quandong), the tree with the round red fruit*, Neville Bonney, Tantanoola, South Australia, 2013

Bruneteau, Jean-Paul, *Tukka: Real Australian food*, Angus & Robertson, Sydney, 1996

Bryant, Simon, *Simon Bryant's Vegies*, Penguin, Melbourne, 2012

Campbell, Rees, *Eat Wild Tasmanian*, Fullers Bookshop, Hobart, 2017

Cherikoff, Vic, *Wild Foods: Looking back 60,000 years for clues to our future survival*, New Holland, Sydney, 2015

Churchill, Dan and Quinn, Hayden, *Surfing the Menu*, Simon & Schuster, Sydney, 2016

Flannery, Tim, *1788/Watkin Tench*, Text Publishing, Melbourne, 2009

Fielke, Andrew, *Australia's Creative Native Cuisine*, Brolly Books, Melbourne, 2020

Gammage, Bill, *The Biggest Estate on Earth: How Aborigines Made Australia*, Allen & Unwin, Sydney, 2011

Gould, Richard A, *Yiwara: Foragers of the Australian Desert*, Charles Scribner's Sons, New York, 1969

Isaacs, Jennifer, *Bush Food: Aboriginal food and herbal medicine*, Ure Smith, Sydney, 1991 (find this and many other of this author's books at <www.jenniferisaacs.com.au>)

Kersh, Jennice and Raymond, *Edna's Table*, Hodder & Stoughton, Sydney, 1998

Langton, Marcia, *Welcome to Country: A travel guide to Indigenous Australia*, Explore Australia, 2018

Low, Tim, *Wild Food Plants of Australia*, HarperCollins, Sydney, 1991

Newton, John, *The Oldest Foods on Earth: A history of Australian native produce*, NewSouth Publishing, Sydney, 2016

Noone, Brian, *Capers: From wild harvest to gourmet food*, Caperplants, 2016 (find at <www.caperplants.com>)

Olszewski, Peter, *A Salute to the Humble Yabby*, Angus & Robertson, Sydney, 1980

Pascoe, Bruce, *Dark Emu: Aboriginal Australia and the Birth of Agriculture*, New Edition, Magabala Books, Broome, 2018

Yunkaporta, Tyson, *Sand Talk: How Indigenous Thinking Can Save the World*, Text, Melbourne, 2019

ONLINE ARTICLES

'Australia: The land where time began – a biography of the Australian continent' <www.austhrutime.com/angiosperms.htm>

'Bigger appetite for kangaroo meat needed to rein in booming roo numbers, ecologist says' <www.abc.net.au/news/2017-09-10/cull-kangaroos-and-eat-their-meat-scientist-urges/8887432>

Behavioral Measures of Neurotoxicity: Report of a Symposium <www.ncbi.nlm.nih.gov/books/NBK234978/>

'Defining the unique flavours of Australian native foods' <www.agrifutures.com.au/publications/defining-the-unique-flavours-of-australian-native-foods>

'How kangaroos could be jeopardising conservation efforts across Australia' <www.theguardian.com/environment/2021/feb/06/how-kangaroos-could-be-jeopardising-conservation-efforts-across-australia>

Kangaroo Conservation <www.theconversation.com/yes-kangaroos-are-endangered-but-not-the-species-you-think-93203>

'Kangaroo population declines in NSW by 4 million, "largely attributed" to drought' <www.abc.net.au/news/2021-02-15/drought-drives-kangaroo-population-decline-in-nsw/13144680>

Nature's Helping Hand <www.avoidglasses.com/natural-cancer-treatment/themaroonbushstory/>

'University study finds economic window for native grains production' <www.sydney.edu.au/news-opinion/news/2020/11/09/university-study-finds-economic-window-for-native-grains-product.html>

Scaevola spinescens (currant bush, maroon bush) <www.omicsonline.org/open-access/phenolic-compounds-antioxidant-and-anticancer-properties-of-the-australian-maroon-bush-scaevola-spinescens-goodeniaceaeod-samples-1948-593X.S12-002.php?aid=36236>.

INDEX

INDEX

INDEX